EDUCATION IN A COMPETITIVE AND GLOBALIZING WORLD SERIES

DISADVANTAGED STUDENTS AND CRISIS IN FAITH-BASED URBAN SCHOOLS

[redacted]

EDUCATION IN A COMPETITIVE AND GLOBALIZING WORLD SERIES

Motivation in Education
Desmond H. Elsworth (Editor)
2009. ISBN: 978-1-60692-234-7

The Reading Literacy of U.S. Fourth-Grade Students in an International Context
Justin Baer, Stéphane Baldi, Kaylin Ayotte, Patricia J. Gree and Daniel McGrath
2009. ISBN: 978-1-60741-138-3

Teacher Qualifications and Kindergartners' Achievements
Cassandra M. Guarino, Laura S. Hamilton, J.R. Lockwood, Amy H. Rathbun and Elvira Germino Hausken
2009. ISBN: 978-1-60741-180-2

Effects of Family Literacy Interventions on Children's Acquisition of Reading
Ana Carolina Pena (Editor)
2009. ISBN: 978-1-60741-236-6

Nutrition Education and Change
Beatra F. Realine (Editor)
2009. ISBN: 978-1-60692-983-4

Reading at Risk: A Survey of Literary Reading in America
Rainer D. Ivanov
2009. ISBN: 978-1-60692-582-9

Evaluating Online Learning: Challenges and Strategies for Success
Arthur T. Weston (Editor)
2009. ISBN: 978-1-60741-107-9

Learning in the Network Society and the Digitized School
Rune Krumsvik (Editor)
2009. ISBN: 978-1-60741-172-7

Rural Education in the 21st Century
Christine M.E. Frisiras (Editor)
2009. ISBN: 978-1-60692-966-7

IT- Based Project Change Management System
Faisal Manzoor Arain
and Low Sui Pheng
2009. ISBN: 978-1-60741-148-2

Reading: Assessment, Comprehension and Teaching
Nancy H. Salas and Donna D. Peyton (Editors)
2009. ISBN: 978-1-60692-615-4

Reading: Assessment, Comprehension and Teaching
Nancy H. Salas and Donna D. Peyton (Editors)
2009. ISBN: 978-1-60876-543-0
(Online Book)

Mentoring: Program Development, Relationships and Outcomes
Michael I. Keel (Editor)
2009. ISBN: 978-1-60692-287-3

Mentoring: Program Development, Relationships and Outcomes
Michael I. Keel (Editor)
2009. ISBN: 978-1-60876-727-4 (Online Book)

Enhancing Prospects of Longer-Term Sustainability of Cross-Cultural INSET Initiatives in China
Chunmei Yan
2009. ISBN: 978-1-60741-615-9

Multimedia in Education and Special Education
Onan Demir and Cari Celik
2009. ISBN: 978-1-60741-073-7

PCK and Teaching Innovations
Syh-Jong Jang
2009. ISBN: 978-1-60741-147-5

Academic Administration: A Quest for Better Management and Leadership in Higher Education
Sheying Chen (Editor)
2009. ISBN: 978-1-60741-732-3

New Research in Education: Adult, Medical and Vocational
Edmondo Balistrieri
and Giustino DeNino (Editors)
2009. ISBN: 978-1-60741-873-3

Approaches to Early Childhood and Elementary Education
Francis Wardle
2009. ISBN: 978-1-60741-643-2

Recent Trends in Education
Borislav Kuzmanović and Adelina Cuevas (Editors)
2009. ISBN: 978-1-60741-795-8

Expanding Teaching and Learning Horizons in Economic Education
Franklin G. Mixon, Jr. and Richard J. Cebula
2009. ISBN: 978-1-60741-971-6

Challenges of Quality Education in Sub-Saharan African Countries
Daniel Namusonge Sifuna and Nobuhide Sawamura
2010. ISBN: 978-1-60741-509-1

Developments in Higher Education
Mary Lee Albertson (Editor)
2010. ISBN: 978-1-60876-113-5

The Process of Change in Education: Moving from Descriptive to Prescriptive Research
Baruch Offir
2010. ISBN: 978-1-60741-451-3

Success in Mathematics Education
Caroline B. Baumann
2009. ISBN: 978-1-60692-299-6

Special Education in the 21st Century
MaryAnn T. Burton (Editor)
2010. ISBN: 978-1-60741-556-5

Collaborative Learning: Methodology, Types of Interactions and Techniques
Edda Luzzatto and Giordano DiMarco (Editors)
2010. ISBN: 978-1-60876-076-3

Voices of Foreign-Born African American Teacher Educators in the United States
Festus E. Obiakor, Patrick Grant and Sunday O. Obi (Editors)
2010. ISBN: 978-1-60876-322-1

Delving into Diversity: An International Exploration of Issues of Diversity in Education
Vanessa Green and Sue Cherrington (Editors)
2010. ISBN: 978-1-60876-361-0

Adopting Blended Learning for Collaborative Work in Higher Education
Alan Hogarth
2010. ISBN: 978-1-60876-260-6

Handbook of Lifelong Learning Developments
Margaret P. Caltone (Editor)
2010. ISBN: 978-1-60876-177-7

Disadvantaged Students and Crisis in Faith-Based Urban Schools
Thomas G. Wilson
2010. ISBN: 978-1- 60741-535-0

Educational Change
Aden D. Henshall and Bruce C. Fontanez (Editors)
2010. ISBN: 978-1-60876-389-4

Career Development
Hjalmar Ohlsson and Hanne Borg (Editors)
2010. ISBN: 978-1-60741-464-3

Virtual Worlds: Controversies at the Frotnier of Education
Kieron Sheehy, Rebecca Ferguson and Gill Clough (Editors)
2010. ISBN: 978-1-60876-261-3

Health Education: Challenges, Issues and Impact
André Fortier and Sophie Turcotte (Editors)
2010. ISBN: 978-1-60876-568-3

Disadvantaged Students and Crisis in Faith-Based Urban Schools
Thomas G. Wilson
2010. ISBN: 978-1-60741-535-0

EDUCATION IN A COMPETITIVE AND GLOBALIZING WORLD SERIES

DISADVANTAGED STUDENTS AND CRISIS IN FAITH-BASED URBAN SCHOOLS

THOMAS G. WILSON
EDITOR

Nova Science Publishers, Inc.
New York

For permission to use material from this book please contact us:
Telephone 631-231-7269; Fax 631-231-8175
Web Site: http://www.novapublishers.com

LIBRARY OF CONGRESS CATALOGING-IN-PUBLICATION DATA

Wilson, Thomas G., 1960-
Disadvantaged students and crisis in faith-based urban schools / author, Thomas G. Wilson.
p. cm.
Includes bibliographical references and index.
ISBN 978-1-60741-535-0 (hardcover)
1. Church schools--United States. 2. Urban schools--United States. 3. Children with social disabilities--Education--United States. I. Title.
LC427.W45 2009
371.071'091732--dc22
2009031974

Published by Nova Science Publishers, Inc. ✣ New York

CONTENTS

PREFACE

According to the National Center for Education Statistics, between the 1999–2000 and 2005–06 school years, the K–12 faith-based education sector lost nearly 1,200 schools and nearly 425,000 students. For generations, these schools have played an invaluable role in America's cities. To lose these schools is to lose a positive, central character in the narrative of urban America. For many urban parents, the moral grounding, community ethic, safe and structured environment, and academic rigor of faith-based schools are invaluable to their children. The underserved children of America's cities deserve access to high-performing educational options. A strong education institution can stabilize a community. A strong school in an underserved community can destabilize fragile social networks, depress job creation and economic development, and exacerbate the collective sense of despair resulting from scarce community resources and opportunities. America's faith-based urban schools—so prized by so many families—are well worth this effort.

This book consists of public domain documents which have been located, gathered, combined, reformatted, and enhanced with a subject index, selectively edited and bound to provide easy access.

In: Disadvantaged Students and Crisis in...
Editor: Thomas G. Wilson

ISBN: 978-1-60741-535-0

Chapter 1

OPENING PRESENTATION

The White House Domestic Policy Council

KARL ZINSMEISTER

I'm Karl Zinsmeister. I'm the President's domestic policy advisor and am very happy to see you all here. And thank you for making time for this important subject this morning.

I want to start by just assuring you that this is a subject that the White House cares deeply about and that specifically the President cares deeply about. Just yesterday actually, I ran into Senator Lamar Alexander who, of course, used to be the Education Secretary before he became Senator. And Lamar told me that the President has been badgering him about how troubling it is that that these faith-based schools in poor neighborhoods are closing. So I was very pleased to learn that I'm not the only one who's receiving Presidential nudges on this topic.

I spoke last night very briefly to some of you about my discomfort with the terms "public schools" and "private schools" as they're conventionally used in the national discourse. And I pointed out that the kind of schools that we are talking about today that are run by faith organizations rather than by the government are in the ways that matter, I think, every bit as much public institutions as the Red Cross or the United Way or the YMCA or any of the other entities that we think of as serving the public good.

The reason we are gathered today under the aegis of the White House is because faith-based schools are not only important to the people who use them, but they are important to the common good of the nation as a whole. I thought it would be useful for me to establish in a little more detail why this is a cause for national concern. A lot of you are already convinced, but I think it's important at a national conference to get that on the record, so I'm going to explain a little bit of the problem here today.

The problem begins with the familiar and very discouraging reality depicted in this figure. Over last 25 years, as we all know, the Federal Government, State and local authorities, lots of businesses, academics, and philanthropists have poured tremendous amounts of attention and resources into our urban public schools. And we've made some very clear progress. There's absolutely no question about that. The achievement gap has closed across racial and ethnic boundaries. But I think we all also know that overall student achievement in our weak inner-city public schools is still abysmally low, unacceptably low.

And this chart you see here is an example of that. Depicted here are the results on the NAEP test, the so-called National Assessment of Educational Progress, which is the definitive national standardized achievement exam. And you can see that only about 22 percent of the eighth-graders in our large inner cities are now proficient or advanced in math (Figure 1). In cities like some of the ones we've listed, the figure is even lower. (For NAEP eighth-grade reading scores, see Figure 8 in the main report.)

Only 52 percent of the students in today's major urban public school districts leave high school with a diploma. Linger on that for a minute. Half of our inner-city children are not graduating, and in some places the figures are worse (see Figure 9 in the main report).

Obviously, this is a devastating problem, and it requires its own mobilization and its own solutions, which is exactly what No Child Left Behind is all about. It's what the charter school movement is all about. It's what school choice is all about. It's what hundreds and hundreds of corporate and philanthropic projects are fighting to overturn. These are big priorities for us, and I think probably for almost everyone in this room.

But in the meantime, while these attempts to fix our public schools are taking place, let us remember a whole generation of children is growing up in these neighborhoods. And today's families in places like Baltimore and Cleveland and Detroit and so forth cannot wait. They cannot wait for these public schools to turn themselves around. They need alternatives for their boys and their girls right now.

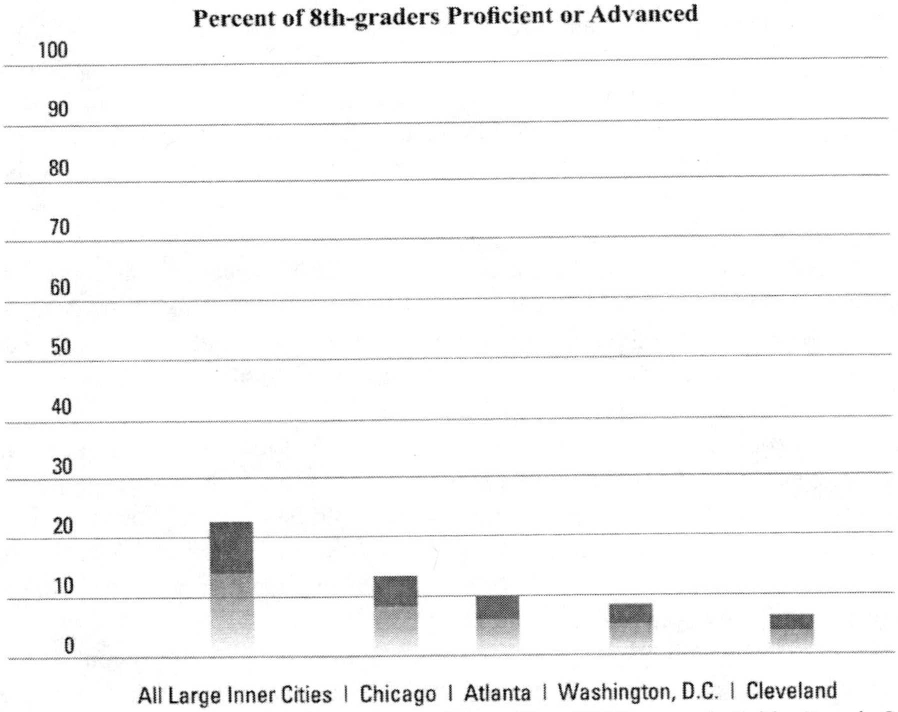

Karl Zinsmeister, "White House Summit on Inner-City Children and Faith Based Schools," (presentation, The White House, Washington, D.C., April 24, 2008).

Figure 1. Math Achievement in Urban Public Schools

In many of our poor neighborhoods, the sole escape hatch, the only viable alternative for families, is the local faith-based school, where somewhat miraculously, educators with a mission have taken many of the very same children who were floundering (in public schools) … and given them direction and stability and skills. That's the most fundamental reason why it's a matter of serious concern for our communities and for our nation, as well as obviously a tragedy for many individual souls that so many of these high-functioning inner-city faith-based schools are now disappearing.

To summarize, our approach to offering quality education for disadvantaged urban kids is … a three-legged stool. None of these legs are failsafe, they're all important, and they can complement each other.

First we need to try to (create) better public education. But I want to remind you that experience has shown this is no simple task. Turning around a failed urban public school is really tough work, extraordinarily difficult. We know that in Maryland, for instance, (only) 16 percent of the schools that enter the "restructuring" category under NCLB emerge from that category successfully. In California the number is just 5 percent. So it's very tough, slow work. (For more on the difficulty of school turnarounds, see "Attempts at Reform" in the main report.)

The second leg of the stool … is to create new schools. As you know, a whole range of new and more effective schools have been created. Sometimes it's just a school within a school. It (can be) a virtual school. Sometimes it's actually a new physical building. Chartering of new schools is one of the very exciting things that we've seen over the last decade and a half. It's led to some extraordinary institutions and breathed new life into the education reform efforts of many, many cities.

While these attempts to fix our public schools are taking place, let us remember that a whole generation of children are growing up in these neighborhoods. And today's families in places like Baltimore and Cleveland and Detroit cannot wait. They cannot wait for these public schools to turn themselves around. They need alternatives for their boys and girls right now.

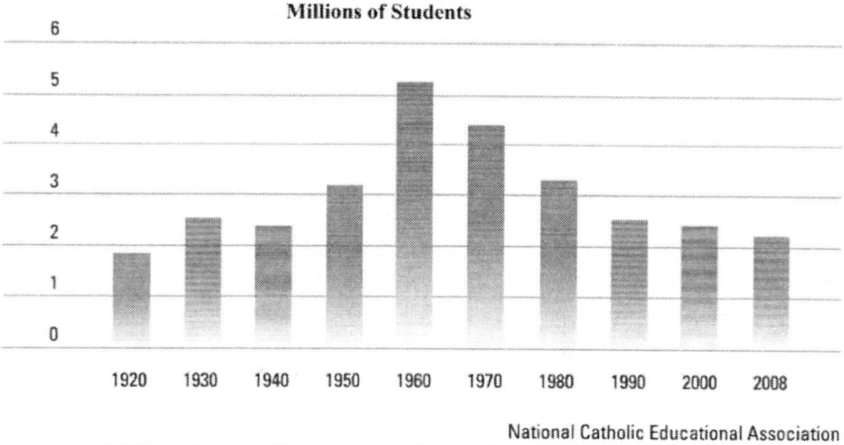

Karl Zinsmeister, "White House Summit on Inner-City Children and Faith Based Schools," (presentation, The White House, Washington, D.C., April 24, 2008).

Figure 2. Catholic School Enrollment in Decline

However, chartering too is not (a) magic bullet. It's very difficult. It's time-consuming and expensive to start new schools. As you know, many States have caps and in many States we are up against those caps, so it's not possible to start new charter schools. And the reality also is that the quality of the charters is inconsistent. Some of them are among the very best schools in the country, and others are achieving only mediocre results.

So that's why we need the third leg of our stool—which is to preserve the excellent schools run by faith organizations that already exist in these (tough) neighborhoods where families really need options. These schools are there. They work. They are desperately needed by the children whose childhood is going to be gone long before the education reform movement reaches their block.

So let us talk a little bit more specifically about faith-based schools. They have very deep roots in this country. They're not a recent phenomenon. We've relied on them from our first days. 1606 was when the first Catholic school was founded in this country. There's a Catholic school in New Orleans, I've been told, still operating today that was opened in 1727. The first Quaker educational institution opened in Philadelphia in 1683. And fully four decades before the American Revolution, there were Jewish day schools operating in New York City (for more, see "Faith-based Schools in America" in the main report).

Faith-based schools have been a very big part our education (system) and continue to be …nearly one of every five K–12 institutions in the country today is faith-based. So these (schools) are providing critical educational services to kids all across the country (see Figure 1 in the main report).

A little more than a third of these are Catholic schools. That's the biggest category, but lots and lots of other faiths are also represented. I was talking to a whole gang of Milwaukee folks last night and will remind you that there are literally scores of Lutheran schools in Milwaukee that have been a very important part of the educational solution in that city. In total, there are more than 4 million children in this country (currently) being educated in faith-based schools.

Nearly one of every five K– 12 institutions in the country today is faith-based.

Let me directly address this issue of whether these alternative schools are somehow out of the mainstream of the American experience… (In 2006) a Harris poll asked people about their actual experience … "What as parents have you done with your own children? What kinds of schools have you sent them to?"

The somewhat startling reality—I don't think this has sunk in with most Americans—is that about four out of 10 American parents today have sent at least one of their children to something other than the traditional public school in their neighborhood. The biggest single (alternative) is faith-based schools. But there are also other private schools in the mix, home schools, and charter schools.[2]

The point I want to make here is that this is not some fringy phenomenon. This is something that four out of 10 parents have executed in their own family lives as being the best solution for their own child. By the way, just as a point of interest … there is also good research out there that shows that in many large cities, (a higher percentage of) public schoolteachers send their own kids to (private) schools (than the general public).[3]

Another related fact to keep in mind is that even today, without any concerted federal effort to (address) this problem, there are about 150,000 kids attending (private) schools (through school choice programs).[4] It's already happening. There are little Federal niche programs; there are some State programs…

So, faith-based schools are a very big and important part of the (American) education landscape. And the largest single provider is the Catholic Church… even back at the time of the Civil War, there were already more than 200 Catholic schools in the U.S.

Professor Viteritti, in the panel I'm going to chair in a minute, will discuss this … Catholic schools expanded rapidly around the turn of the century (and) were very important in assimilating wave after wave of immigrants from places like Italy and Poland and Ireland (see the Summit Presentation of Joseph Viteritti in the appendix). And during the last century, the number of Catholic schools reached their peak … (around) 1960 with 13,000 Catholic schools. And at that point there were more than 5 million kids in Catholic schools (see note 8 in the main report).

And then the decline started (see The Loss of Urban Faith-based Schools in the main report). (Since) reaching their high-water mark in 1960, (these) schools began to decline … more than 5,000 Catholic schools have closed nationwide. (see Figure 2 and Figure 4 in the main report).

Enrollment today in terms of bodies (rather than) schools…is about half what it was at the peak. And alas, this trend is continuing … in just the last eight years, nearly 1,200 Catholic schools were closed or consolidated, and (most) of those were located in America's inner cities ….

(Figure 4 in the main report) shows some of the cities that have been (especially) hard hit … Chicago has lost 66 schools (and) Detroit 63. This is only (since) 1998, mind you … just the last 10 years … (This) pattern applies … not only to Catholic schools (but also to other faith-based schools in inner cities) …

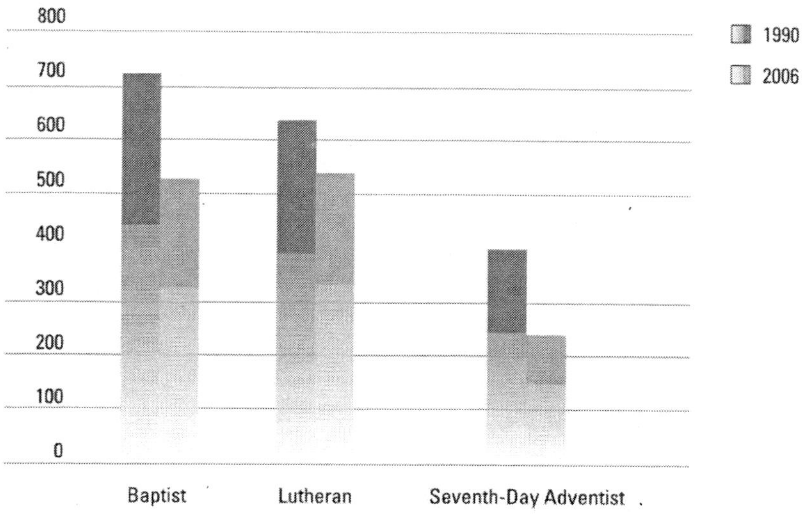

Karl Zinsmeister, "White House Summit on Inner-City Children and Faith Based Schools,"(presentation, The White House, Washington, D.C., April 24, 2008).

Figure 3. Other Faith-based Schools Are Also in Decline in Urban Areas

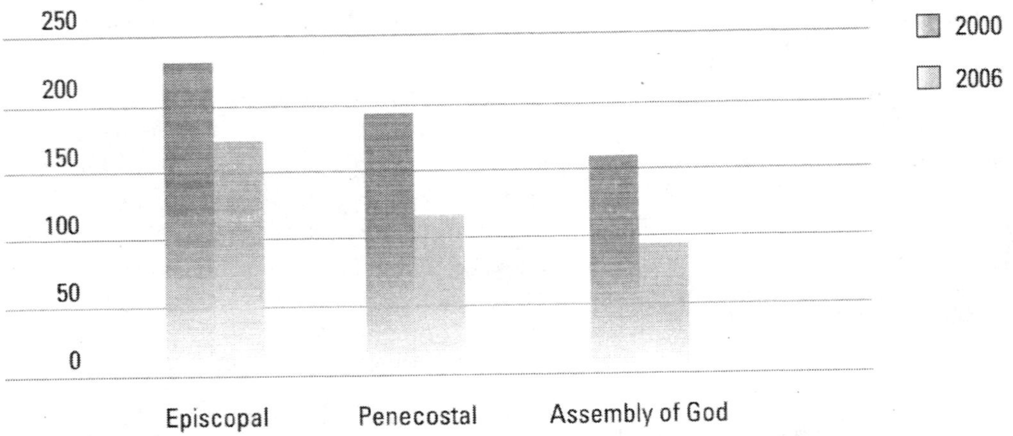

Karl Zinsmeister, "White House Summit on Inner-City Children and Faith Based Schools," (presentation, The White House, Washington, D.C., April 24, 2008).

Figure 4. Even Schools That Bucked the Trend Are Now Closing

Baptist schools have had a big decline…Lutheran schools are down, Seventh-day Adventist schools (are closing) (see Figure 3). There were a few Protestant schools…that bucked the trend for a while, (holding) steady or even (managing) to grow up into the 1990s. But now they're also declining.

Since 2000—so this is the last six years—Episcopal schools are down; Pentecostal (and) Assembly of God schools (are down). Since 2000, the last six years, we've lost about 200 urban schools run by just these three denominations (see Figure 4).

The cumulative losses (can be seen in Table 1 in the main report). You can see that it's about 1,200 schools of various faiths representing 425,000 kids. That's the number that got my attention. If those lost faith-based schools were considered one school district, it would be the second biggest school district in the country, after only New York City. That's just what we've lost in the last six years…

What we are focusing on here is specifically faith-based inner-city schools. As you can see from (Figure 6 and 7 in the main report), private schools in general are doing fine. Faith-based schools in general are doing fine. The problem is faith-based schools in poor urban neighborhoods. That's what we are focused on. That's what the White House is concerned about…

(Inner cities is) where the problem is worst, but it's also where the children are most in need, most lacking alternatives, most (in) need (of) a safe and caring and academically rigorous alternative because their public schools tend to be so troubled and because those families don't have the means to necessarily exercise other options.

Why should we care (about these losses)? If this is just…consumer choice at work and people are migrating and voting with their feet—why should we care? One reason we care is because these schools have very particular and (positive) effects (on) inner-city populations. As William Jeynes is going to talk about in greater detail in the next panel, faith-based schools are serving these students very well, especially students who have been let down by their public schools. And in the process, they're doing us all a favor by making sure that instead of becoming unproductive dropouts, these are children can join the American mainstream…

Compared to other students of the same demographic background, minority students in urban Catholic schools are 42 percent likelier to complete high school, and inner-city minorities are two and a half times more likely to obtain a college degree if they attended a Catholic rather than a public high school, so very impressive results (see, for example, note 25 in the main report).

Inner cities are where the children are most in need and most lacking alternatives. Their public schools tend to be the most troubled and their families don't have the means to exercise other options.

And not only do they manage to achieve excellence—one of the (most) important goals of education—but they (also score well in terms of equality)…The classic book on this was *Catholic Schools and the Common Good* by Anthony Bryk and (Lee and Holland). They pointed out that not only do these schools achieve relatively high levels of learning, but as they put it, "they distribute this learning more equitably with regard to race and class than in the public sector" (see note 22 in the main report).

Part of the explanation it appears – again, this is a little bit of a mystery – to be the school culture; that these institutions outperform others at…creating discipline and safety and racial harmony and a sense that all children can succeed. Faith-based schools have also been shown to inspire very high levels of teacher commitment and of student engagement.

The bottom line when you put it all together is pretty startling:…the (graduation rate) of students in faith-based high schools is in the high 90s, even in these tough neighborhoods, and the proportion that go on to college is also in the high 90s.[5] I just want to remind you that the national average for public high schools is about 70 percent, and in these cities where these schools are concentrated, it's more like 50 percent (see Figure 9 in the main report). So (faith-based urban schools) are really (accomplishing) remarkable achievements.

Which brings us to our next question: If these (schools are) educationally successful, why are so many of them closing? It is a reality that these places are successful, that they are popular, that they have been in their neighborhoods for generations, that there's an appetite for their services. The problem is their business model, and there are several explanations, (of which) three rise above the others.

The first is the blockage of government aid. Unlike public schools, obviously, and unlike private schools in other industrial nations, U.S. faith-based schools are blocked from receiving most streams of government education aid. Some States provide transportation or funding for textbooks, and there are even some federal funds that get passed on for (services for) poor students and students with special needs…But, in general, direct government financial support to these schools has been denied.

Charles Glenn is going to comment (on this) in this first panel. He'll point out to you that this is pretty unusual (internationally), that the U.S. is really the outlier in this area. In countries like Denmark and Belgium and Australia and France, the reality is that the government funds the parent's choice of schools wherever it may take the child, including into faith-based settings. But for a variety of peculiar historical reasons which I hope Joseph Viteritti is going to unpack for us in this first panel, for a variety of reasons this has not been the case in our country. So government aid is one big problem.

Another big problem is the population shifts that have (transformed American) cities over the last generation. The middle-class and working-class blue-collar families that have traditionally been very heavily served by these faith-based schools have mostly migrated out of cities. There aren't many left, and this has reduced the size and vitality of many of these urban congregations. Fewer families obviously also mean fewer students, and fewer families mean less church income, which is terribly important to subsidizing the operation of these schools.

Detroit

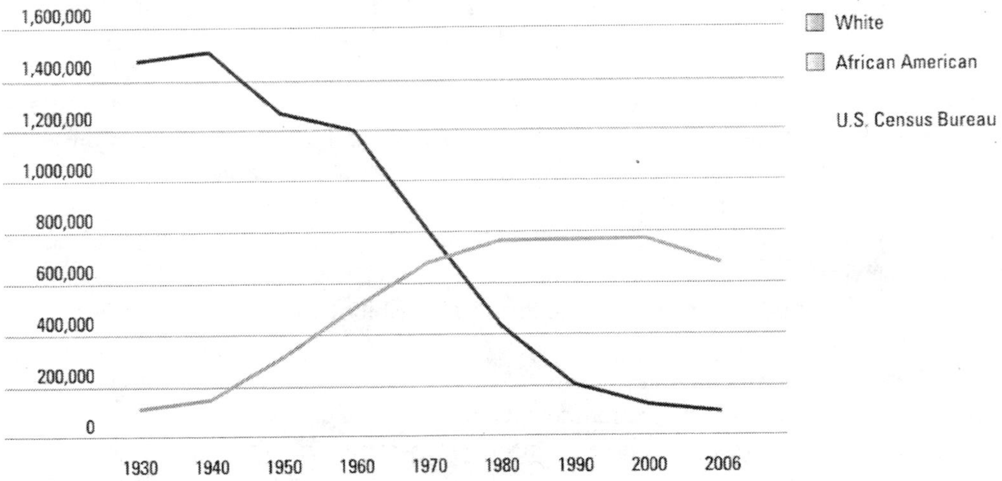

Philadelphia

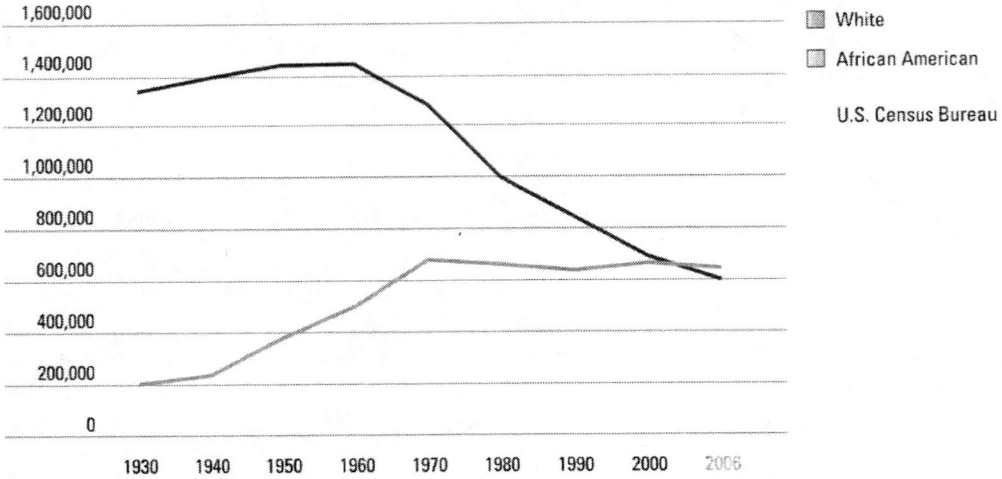

Changes in the U.S. Catholic School Population Since 1970:

Minorities: Up 250 percent National Catholic Educational Association

Non-Catholics: Up 500 percent

Karl Zinsmeister, "White House Summit on Inner-City Children and Faith Based Schools," (presentation, The White House, Washington, D.C., April 24, 2008),

Figure 5. Serving New Populations and All Religions

This chart (Figure 5) illustrates (these demographic changes). The important part of this slide is (at) the bottom... Since 1970 the minority population in Catholic schools has increased 250 percent, and the non-Catholic population in Catholic schools has increased by 500 percent.

So here in Washington, D.C., for instance, there are 13 Catholic schools in the Archdiocese that are 95 percent or more minority. So this is an important new mission of (schools) in these neighborhoods...

And low-income families are going to have less ability to pay tuition...As a result, they put more of a demand on churches and on the donors.

> **Faith-based urban schools are keeping their tuition at very modest levels. But setting tuition at such low levels means that the cost of these schools is obviously a lot higher than their income. Plenty of these schools have literally six-figure or even seven-figure annual subsidy requirements. So you can see why lots of them live on the knife's edge.**

Catholic and other religious schools are keeping their tuition levels very modest (see Figure 10 in the main report)—(generally) in the $3,000 to $3,500 per year range. Other (private) schools (average) more than about twice that. The tuition at a typical faith-based elementary school today covers about 60 percent of the costs. The rest is kicked in by church subsidies or gifts, and at high schools the typical tuition covers about 80 percent of the costs. (As a result, higher enrollment actually means) bigger deficits.

This is unlike other businesses where every new customer is (financially) good. In this business, every new customer is wonderful from the point of view of social justice, but each one arrives with a big net subsidy requirement...Setting tuition at such low levels means that the cost of these schools is a lot higher than their income. Plenty of these schools (have) literally six-figure or even seven-figure annual subsidy requirements, so you can see why lots of them live on a knife's edge.

The third factor that affects the business model of these schools is staff costs...The nuns and priests who are no longer in these schools (have been) replaced by lay teachers, and those teachers have to be paid (see Figure 11 in the main report). The salary for an experienced teacher in New York City these days in the public schools is about $85,000 (see note 107 in the main report). That's what other schools have to match if they're going to get the bodies, and it's a heavy burden.

So this is the bottom line (see Figure 6) ... You have very little government aid. You have increasing demand for church subsidies. You've got an increasingly low-income student body, and as a result, the schools are trying to hold their tuition below cost...And then the rising teacher salaries we talked about.

It's easy to see why lots of faith-based schools are in financial crisis today. (But) no one intended this. There's been no sabotage. No one purposely set up this confluence of events. But it's nonetheless a very serious problem.

Let me close by pointing out that President Bush is not the first President to take an interest in this subject. (The following) is a quotation from a (Presidential) panel... back in 1972: "If the decline continues, pluralism in education will cease, parental options will virtually terminate, and public schools will have to absorb millions of students. The greatest impact will be on large urban centers, with especially grievous consequences for poor and middle-and lower-middle-class families in racially changing neighborhoods, where the nearby nonpublic school is an indispensable stabilizing factor." (For more, see Figure 3 in the main report.)

So alas, this is not a new problem. It is, however, a deep and continuing problem. And the sad news is that literally millions of seats have been lost in these schools since those words were written. But the good news is that this day is going to give us some ideas as to how we might turn around that trend line. So with that, I will invite our participants in our first panel to come up and join me on stage, and we'll get started.

Little government aid

+

Growing demand for church subsidies

+

Increasingly low-income student body

+

Holding tuition below cost

+

Rising teacher salaries

Financial Crisis

Karl Zinsmeister, "White House Summit on Inner-City Children and Faith Based Schools," (presentation, The White House, Washington, D.C., April 24, 2008).

Figure 6. Consequence

In: Disadvantaged Students and Crisis in...
Editor: Thomas G. Wilson

ISBN: 978-1-60741-535-0

Chapter 2

PANEL I: FAITH-BASED SCHOOLS AND THE COMMON GOOD

The White House Domestic Policy Council

KARL ZINSMEISTER

This is our academic panel. We have a dean. We have a college president. We have two distinguished professors with us. Since we are meeting in the Reagan Building, I cannot help but remind you that Ronald Reagan's definition of an academic was a person who sees something happen in practice and wonders if it would work in theory.

But this is not the kind of academic who comes to (this) White House summit...In all seriousness these are researchers who have observed faith-based schools for years and years. They have become national authorities in understanding how these schools work and what they do for the nation. I'm going to introduce them in reverse order...

Our final speaker is going to be the Reverend Floyd Flake, who is a senior pastor at Greater Allen Cathedral in New York, one of the really great American churches, (located) in Queens... In addition, Reverend Flake is president of Wilberforce University in Ohio.

He was also a congressman for a little less than a dozen years. And back when I was a journalist, Congressman Flake was the kind of political figure you delighted to cross paths with because he wasn't robotically predictable like a lot of political figures can become. He didn't have that little tape recorder in his head that just turned on and said all the expected things. When you asked him a question, you (could) actually get some spontaneous honesty out of him. He also crossed (political and ideological) boundaries in some very interesting ways that made him one of the more interesting Members of Congress.

The third speaker today is going to be William Jeynes. William Jeynes is a professor of education at California State University and also affiliated as a scholar with Baylor University, which some of you may know has been snapping up some very interesting and idiosyncratic scholars from all parts of the country over the last few years, and Dr. Jeynes is part of that.

He's written numerous books and articles on religious education and educational history, most recently a book entitled *American Educational History: Schools, Society, and the*

Common Good. And he is a graduate of Harvard University and University of Chicago and has three children.

Our second speaker is going to be Joseph Viteritti, who is a professor at Hunter College in New York and also the director of the graduate program there in urban affairs. His most recent of nine books and lots and lots of articles is called *The Last Freedom: Religion from the Public School to the Public Square.* He also has toiled in the vineyards of actual practice and served as an assistant to the chancellor of schools in New York, Boston, and San Francisco, so he has practical experience as well.

And our first speaker is going to be Charles Glenn, who is the interim dean and professor at Boston University School of Education.

I had the good fortune to cross paths with Dr. Glenn back when I was running (a current affairs) magazine, and he coauthored a story for us that was a fascinating glimpse into how other countries finance education. He is the U.S. authority on this topic, and I will note that he is the one who first educated me on this idea that there is an international standard out there that allows parents to choose their school (with) public funding to follow. The United States is one of the few countries that doesn't adhere to this standard. So let us start with Dr. Glenn.

CHARLES GLENN

Thank you. I want to make four points. The first, as Karl has already mentioned, is that clearly the right of parents to choose the schools that children attend is an internationally accepted norm. Every country in the world except North Korea, Vietnam, and Cuba, allows parents to choose schools. Every western democracy except the United States provides public funding to support those choices.

As you all know, I think, under a decision of the Supreme Court in 1925, that right of parents to choose schools is recognized in American law as well. But there's a fundamental equity issue in the American situation in that parents who lack the resources to support nongovernment education for their children, are not able to exercise the right that they possess under those international norms. The various international covenants for human rights spell out clearly that this is a fundamental human right, and the United Nations and UNESCO have both agreed that it is fundamental in vindicating the right to education that the education provided not only be adequate, but that it be acceptable to parents.

Every country in the world except North Korea, Vietnam, and Cuba, allows parents to choose schools. Every western democracy except the United States provides public funding to support those choices...There's a fundamental equity issue in the American situation in that parents who lack the resources to support nongovernment education for their children are not able to exercise the right that they possess under international norms.

The second point I want to make is that in all of these other countries which fund the schools that parents choose, religious schools are among those that are funded. In fact, in almost all cases, religious schools are the majority of the schools that government funds in addition to its own schools.

For example, in the Netherlands about 30 percent of the elementary children attend Catholic schools. About 30 percent attend Protestant schools. About 30 percent attend local government schools. And the other 10 percent attend a variety of schools, whether Waldorf or Islamic schools or Jewish schools. And all of those schools, 100 percent, are all funded completely by government. And that is regarded by the Dutch as a fundamental act of justice to ensure that every parent has the opportunity to attend a school that he or she can have full confidence in.

The reason that's not the case in the United States is the 19th-century hostility toward Catholic immigrants. And this is, of course, a uniquely distinctive issue in the United States. In Australia, where there were also many Catholic immigrants, as part of a political accommodation of those immigrants, the Australian government in fact funds Catholic and other nongovernment schools. And a high proportion of pupils in Australia, as in Canada, as in France, as in Germany, as in England, attend schools with a religious character.

In all of these other countries which fund the schools that parents choose, religious schools are among those that are funded.

This has not—and this is my third point—caused conflict within these countries. It's often feared – we are often told, including by members of the Supreme Court who should know better, that if you fund religious schools, this will have the effect of causing religious conflict within the society. In fact, the historical record is very clear about that. In a number of countries, there was bitter conflict over schooling until government began to fund whatever schools parents wished to have their children attend.

Just to mention Netherlands again, there was—for 70 years the political issue around which the Dutch common people were mobilized and the first political parties were founded was a so-called "schoolstrijd," the battle over the schools. That battle was resolved in 1917 when the constitution was amended to guarantee equal funding, equal support—and this will lead to my fourth point, a guarantee of the distinctiveness of schools—and then the battle over the schools went away.

And the Dutch, in fact, as you know are famously tolerant. Arguably to some of us, perhaps they're too tolerant in some ways. But you do not see and you have not seen mobs of Catholics and Protestants killing each other in the streets because 30 percent of the children attend Catholic schools and 30 percent attend Protestant schools.

The only country that might seem an exception to that would be Northern Ireland, where of course there has been a long and bitter history of Protestant and Catholic conflict, but we all know that that conflict has deeper roots that are not derived from the fact that the government funds Catholic schools in Northern Ireland just as it does in so many other countries.

And then lastly as I said, is the question of the distinctiveness of schools. The issue which often is a matter of concern and should be a matter of concern is whether, with government support, comes government regulation in ways that will remove the distinctiveness, the ability of schools to maintain their integrity, to carry out their mission, in a way that the school and those who sponsor the school define. Or is it necessary that with the government funding comes conformity to the ways in which the public schools operate?

We have to be very careful at a policy level and at a legal level to provide the kinds of protections that...provide for what we could call a freedom of conscience on the part of schools, because if schools are no longer able to be distinctive, then the right of parents to choose schools becomes meaningless.

It seems to me that's a fundamental policy question, one of enormous interest which my Belgian colleague and I have now looked at in more than 50 countries to try to see how different countries have managed that very delicate question of ensuring that schools can maintain their mission, can still be distinctive, can still follow a vision of education, can still have what the French call "distinctive character" and at the same time receive public support.

This issue plays itself out of course in country after country. But the common experience has been, in my judgment, that when those who sponsor schools with a distinctive faith mission or a distinctive pedagogical mission like a Waldorf or a Montessori school, when they remain clear about what it is they are seeking to accomplish, when they ensure that the teachers that they employ share that vision, when they make very clear to parents who are preparing to entrust their children to the school what it is the school does and stands for, when those things happen, schools are able to maintain their distinctiveness even as they receive government support.

So that in the last analysis, the question of distinctiveness, the question of maintaining that clear vision and mission remains in the hands of those who in fact share in the shaping of the individual school's mission. At the same time, however, we have to be very careful at a policy level and at a legal level to provide the kinds of protections that I mentioned that the Dutch Constitution provides for what we could call a freedom of conscience on the part of schools because if schools are no longer able to be distinctive, then the right of parents to choose schools becomes meaningless.

So those four points: This (America's non-funding of nongovernment schools) is not an international norm. Religious schools are commonly funded. The fact that religious schools and nongovernment schools are funded has not caused social division. And finally, the question of the regulation and protection of the distinctiveness of schools is a basic policy question both for government and also for those who are directly engaged in the life of those schools.

JOSEPH VITERITTI

The history of faith-based schools in the inner-city is very largely but not entirely a story about Catholic schools. The subtext of the story involves some very basic American values like liberty, equality, and opportunity.

Catholic schools began in the 19th century in the spirit of protest. At the time public schools were requiring Bible reading, school prayers, and the singing of hymns, all in the Protestant tradition, and Catholic school bishops demanded that either these practices be discontinued or they be provided assistance to open their own schools. This never happened, of course.

In 1875, Congressman James Blaine of Maine tried to pass a constitutional amendment that would have prohibited aid to religious schools. Blaine at the time was trying to cultivate anti-Catholic animosity in an attempt to run for President. The proposal got a majority of votes in both houses of Congress, but it failed. It came four votes short of a supermajority that was needed to pass a constitutional amendment. Many States followed up, though, by passing their own Blaine Amendments, and today Blaine Amendments exist in two-thirds of the State constitutions.

Throughout the 20th century, Catholic schools continued to educate the children and grandchildren of immigrants from Europe, mostly from Ireland and Italy and Poland and Germany, but these were hardly schools of privilege. They scraped by because they were able to get some support in the local collection boxes. They scraped by because they had an army of religious orders that provided cheap labor. But they were very rarely prosperous schools.

I can remember my first-grade class where a young nun sat in front of a roomful of 65 boys from the local tenements and tried to keep order, and she actually did a pretty good job. Catholic education reached its peak in 1965 with 13,000 schools that educated five-and-a-half million children. Suburbanization took many of these students away from the cities and emptied the schools. It also depleted collection boxes. By 1983, Catholic schools had lost half their population.

These schools were subsequently filled by other children, which tended to come from African-American and Hispanic families, who were even less privileged than the children who preceded them and were even less likely to support the schools. Many of them were not Catholics, but there was a place for these students because the religious orders that ran the schools had a philosophy that "We don't educate poor children because they are Catholic. We educate them because we are Catholic."

The market logic doesn't make sense for those who want a religious education but cannot afford it, because you cannot have a private education or a parochial school education if you're poor, unless generosity is provided by philanthropy.

The dawn of the 21st century brought new opportunities and new challenges. In the 1990s, voucher programs were passed in Milwaukee and Cleveland with very strong support from the African-American community that was becoming more and more frustrated with the quality of public education. Support among African-Americans at the time, decades after *Brown's* promise that each child was entitled to an equal education, accentuated the fact that private and parochial schools could be used as a means to serve the cause of educational opportunity. Subsequent voucher programs in Florida and Colorado were struck down by the courts, but fortunately a very vibrant program continues to exist in the District of Columbia.

The new century also brought the growth of charter schools. Charter schools now exist in 40 States. There are 4,100 of them educating 1.2 million people. These charter schools are able to provide alternatives to public schools without charging tuition and as a result have further depleted enrollment in faith-based schools.

Between 2000 and 2007, 780 Catholic schools closed. There seems to be a basic market logic to this that as it all sorted out, children who were interested in the secular benefits of a parochial school education would find their way to charter schools and those who really wanted a religious education would find their way into the remaining religious schools. But the market logic doesn't make sense for those who want a religious education but cannot afford it, because as we speak today, you cannot have a private education or a parochial school education if you're poor, unless generosity is provided by philanthropy (for more on this point, see the Summit presentation of Charles Glenn in the appendix).

This affects not only Catholic schools, but Lutheran schools, Jewish day schools, Christian schools, Islamic schools, and what I would call black independent schools. One of the great tragedies of current policies that do not provide aid to children who attend religious schools is that it undermines the role of the African-American church as a resource in the inner-city.

No institution has more to offer to the development, the healthy development of young African-American children as the black church, and many pastors have attempted to build schools. Reverend Flake, my friend from New York, will tell you more about that later (see the Summit presentation of Reverend Floyd Flake in the appendix). But these schools face the same financial dilemmas as any other school that is dependent on tuition and tries to educate disadvantaged populations.

In 2002, the Supreme Court approved the school voucher program in Cleveland, lifting the constitutional ban on aid to religious schools. But two years later it handed down a decision that again said that States were able to set their own standards for separation between church and State, leaving in place the Blaine amendments that exist in about two-thirds of our States. But this decision may eventually be overturned.

But the real obstacle to aid to religious schools is a political one, and this politics is based on our very real national consensus that we cannot afford to educate children in both public and religious schools. We don't have enough money. It raises serious questions about national priorities. And as Charlie just said, it's a rather unique position for a democracy.

The choice debate will continue. One of the unfortunate outcomes of this debate is that it separates two populations of educators who are very committed to the children they serve—and the children they serve are very much the same children. In the short run I'm not optimistic about changes in public policy that will allow aid to religious schools. This means that the future of faith-based education in the inner-city is going to rely on private philanthropy (for more, see "Philanthropy" in the main report).

Those who step up to the plate in this area should be reminded that the great majority of children who live in cities will continue to attend public schools. The future of urban education and the dialogue about that future should not be treated as competition between two camps. It should not pit one population of disadvantaged children against the other. The point is that all children are our children and that all children deserve a decent education.

William Jeynes

Good day. My name is William Jeynes, and today I'm going to be sharing with you the academic contributions of faith-based schools. And I'm going to show you, first of all, an overview of the foundational research and then the research results on the religious school advantage and thirdly, how public schools may be able to learn from faith-based schools.

First, in terms of an overview of the foundational research, the influence of religious schools and the consistent advantage that students from these schools have had over their counterparts academically in public schools have gone on for some years as means of debate (see "Academic Benefits of Faith-based Schools" in the main report). One of the major contributors to this debate was James Coleman.

He and his colleagues wrote a book entitled *Public and Private High Schools* in which they observed that students from these schools consistently outperformed their counterparts in public schools; but beyond that, they also asserted a number of the reasons behind this difference. And two of the prominent reasons they mentioned were the religious culture of these schools, number one, and also the fact that these schools maintain higher scholastic standards than are typically found in the public schools.

More recently, authors such as Anthony Bryk and others have noted that private religious schools can have an effect well beyond the bounds of their walls into the broader educational landscape, especially as public school leaders are willing to imitate many of the rubrics employed by private religious schools. But what is so notable is that students from private religious schools, even when controlling for socioeconomic status, well outperform their counterparts in public schools.

Faith-based schools reduce both the racial achievement gap and the socio-economic achievement gap by 2 percent.

Second, I want share with you research results on the religious school advantage. Now, if you're going to examine the religious school advantage, it's very important not to examine simply one or two studies, but ideally you want to examine all of them. And fortunately there is a statistical method through which this can be done called meta-analysis. A meta-analysis statistically combines all the relevant existing studies on a given subject in order to determine the aggregated results of such research. So I undertook a meta-analysis to get an overall sense of what the body of research indicates about a religious school advantage, and the results I'm about to present to you.

I was specifically interested in how religious schools addressed the achievement gap. To what extent do faith-based schools reduce the achievement gap? Well, the results I found were truly exciting. That is, if you examine the achievement gap that exists between African-American and white students, that achievement gap is reduced by 25 percent in faith-based schools.

(percentage score advantages)

	African American & Latino Students	White Students
Reading	+8.2%	+6.0%
Math	+8.3%	+6.0%
Social Studies	+8.3%	+5.8%
Science	+6.0%	+4.2%
Test Composite	+8.3%	+6.0%
Left Back	+5.1%	+3.7%
Basic Core	+8.3%	+6.5%

William Jeynes, "White House Summit on Inner-City Children and Faith Based Schools," (presentation, The White House, Washington, D.C., April 24, 2008).

Figure 7. Effects for Attending Religious Schools Versus Public Schools on the Academic Achievement of Twelfth Graders by Race

And also if you examine the achievement gap that typically exists between high socioeconomic students and low socioeconomic students, this achievement gap also is reduced by 25 percent.

Now this is truly exciting, especially because the achievement gap is perhaps the most debated topic in this nation today. We have tried for decades as a nation to reduce the achievement gap with limited success. And to the extent that faith-based schools are a means to reduce students' achievement gap, then the data that I'm presenting really need a very hard look.

I also examined the extent to which students of low socioeconomic status did better in private religious schools than their counterparts in public schools and found that the advantage held no matter what level of school you were talking about, whether it was the high school level, the middle school level, or the elementary school level.

In addition to using meta-analysis to examine the religious school advantage, I have also used nationwide data sets. Principally I have used the National Education Longitudinal Study, which is the most respected data set in education. It consists of about 25,000 students who are a nationally representative group, and through this I examined the religious school advantage.

These data that I am presenting to you are extremely exciting (Figure 7). They show in the left column the results for African-American and Latino students and then in the right column the results for white students. These are the effects of attending religious schools versus public schools on the academic achievement of 12th-graders by race.

And we see that for both groups of these students each outperforms their counterparts in public school. So in other words, in the left-hand column, we see that African-American and Latino students in faith-based schools outperform African-American and Latino students in public schools by 8.2 percent in reading scores. And white students in private religious schools outperform white students in public schools by 6 percent in reading. So we see that the advantages hold for all the races examined.

But there's also something else very important to note from this table. Not only do both groups of students gain by attending private religious schools, but notice very consistently, no matter what academic measure you look at, African-American and Latino students benefit more by attending private religious schools than do white students

(percentage score advantages)

	Lowest SES Quartile	2nd Lowest	2nd Highest Quartile	Highest Quartile
Reading	+7.6%	+6.8%	+5.8%	+5.2%
Math	+7.0%	+6.2%	+5.6%	+5.0%
Social Studies	+6.8%	+5.8%	+5.2%	+4.6%
Science	+5.4%	+4.0%	+3.4%	+3.2%
Test Composite	+7.8%	+6.6%	+5.4%	+4.8%
Left Back	+5.8%	+5.0%	+4.4%	+3.8%
Basic Core	+8.2%	+6.6%	+5.8%	+5.2%

William Jeynes, "White House Summit on Inner-City Children and Faith Based Schools," (presentation, The White House, Washington, D.C., April 24, 2008).

Figure 8. Effects for Attending Religious Schools Versus Public Schools on the Academic Achievement of Twelfth Graders by SES Quartile

Notice, for example, for reading that African-American and Latino students do better than their counterparts by 8.2 percent. For white students, the difference is 6 percent. For math African-American and Latino students have an advantage of 8.3 percent, whites 6 percent and so on.

So no matter whether you look at social studies, science, test composite, whether a student is left behind a grade or whether they take a basic set of courses recommended by the National Assessment of Educational Progress or going on to college, no matter what academic measure you look at, students from faith-based schools, the ones that are performing the best and gaining the most by attending these schools are African-American and Latino students.

And this is extremely important because these are the students that we were trying as a society to help the most, so these results are especially noteworthy. And even if you control for socioeconomic status, again you see the same pattern. No matter what academic measure you look at, the people who benefit the most by attending private religious schools are African-American and Latino students.

Now if these results are exciting, the results I'm about to present are equally exciting, perhaps even more exciting (Figure 8). What I did is I divided students from this national data set into socioeconomic quartiles. I examined the lowest socioeconomic quartile, the second-lowest socioeconomic quartile, all the way up to the highest socioeconomic quartile. And the results indicate that the students who benefit the most by attending private religious schools are those of the lowest socioeconomic quartile.

Once again, it doesn't matter what academic measure you examine; you see the same pattern. So, for example, you see on the screen that for reading tests, students in the lowest socioeconomic quartile had an advantage of 7.6 percent over students in public schools. And then we see students from the second lowest socioeconomic quartile. The advantage there is 6.8 percent. And the higher you go up the socioeconomic ladder, the smaller the difference becomes.

We see basically the same pattern for math scores. The advantage for those of the lowest socioeconomic quartile: 7 percent. They benefit the most. Those of the second-lowest economic quartile, they benefit the second most and so forth. And again you see the same pattern, whether you examine social science scores, science scores, test composite, being left back a grade, or whether students get the basic core set of courses.

So once again, the students who benefit the most by attending private religious schools are those of the lowest socioeconomic quartile. Those who benefit the second most are those from the second lowest socioeconomic quartile. And once again, given that these are the students we are trying to benefit the most, this should cause people to take a second look at the effects of faith-based schools. They are truly doing important work, an important service to our nation.

The positive influence of faith-based schools on achievement grows as students' socioeconomic condition falls. The more disadvantaged the student, the more value provided by a faith-based K–12 education.

Now, we need to examine why it is that attending religious schools reduces the achievement gap. And again, turning to the results of the meta-analysis, if you combine all these studies together, there are basically three trends that you see in the research that has been done. First of all, better school culture: typically people believe the religious schools have a better school culture than one finds in public schools. Second, faith-based schools encourage student religious commitment. And third, faith-based schools encourage parental involvement. These are the three trends that you see in the meta-analysis.

Now, the idea of there being a better school culture is also supported in the National Education Longitudinal Study. For example, first, religious schools are more likely to have racial harmony. There are fewer racial fights, and also they're considered to be more racially friendly by the students.

Second, we notice that religious schools are less likely to have gang problems. Third, we see that religious schools are more likely to have teachers who are interested in students. And finally religious school students are less likely to be offered illegal drugs.

There is also a considerable amount of research on the influence of school choice. Research by Howell and Peterson has examined three different communities that have used voucher programs and found that achievement was higher among religious private school students in those voucher programs and also that parents and students enjoyed these schools better than the public schools. We see basically the same results that have emerged although to a lesser extent in the Milwaukee school choice program and also in European school choice programs.

The third point that I will make is that public schools may be able to learn from faith-based schools. And again the meta-analyses that I have done indicate that there are four items especially that public schools may want to take note of in terms of employing some of the private religious school rubrics. Number one: the importance of maintaining high expectations for students. Number two: the salience of moral education, and moral education does not have to be religious, just the teaching of right and wrong. Third, emphasizing loving and caring teachers. And fourth, encouraging parental involvement.

Now a lot of what I share you may react to by saying, "Well, that's only according to common sense." "Certainly makes sense to me," you might say. But we need to remember what Voltaire said. What Voltaire said was "Common sense is not so common." And I think we have an opportunity as a nation and as people gathered together in this forum today to really make a difference as we encourage and espouse the flourishing of private religious schools.

Horace Mann once said, "Be ashamed to die until you have won some victory for humanity." And I believe today as we encourage the flourishing of private religious schools, we have an opportunity to win a victory for humanity. Thank you very much for your time.

REVEREND FLOYD FLAKE

Thank you, and let us give thanks for all the other speakers. And somewhere it's said the first shall be last, and the last shall be first. And whatever that means this morning, I'm happy to be here and representing the categories that were part of my introduction, but I think the most important category that gives definition to my presence has to do with the founding of a faith-based school 25 years ago.

As the founder of that school, in looking at some of what Charles has said, some of what Bill has said, and certainly some of what Joe has said, the realities are that there is a serious struggle as it relates to the ability to maintain such schools, given that there is such an inequality in terms of the access to resources to make those schools operate and function in a manner that is competitive.

Failing public schools put a great deal of pressure, not only on the system, but also on communities. It puts pressure on families, and when families have an opportunity for an alternative such as a faith-based institution, they make the choice.

The school we built 25 years ago for pre-K through eighth-graders has been extremely successful from a competitive perspective. And the reason for and rationale for continued existence is the fact that our responsibility to prepare young people for global competitiveness can only be done when people are willing to make the necessary sacrifices to bring about the means by which these young people do not feel as if they will never have the ability to be in a position where they will be able to compete economically.

Economic standing then in many instances rises based on the ability to have the educational foundations that are often found in those institutions that we consider to represent something outside the fabric of what we define as public education. Those definitions that we give are generally so limited that it does not open the door for an inclusion of institutions like mine and those that surround me, most of which are Catholic.

What we have discovered over the years as we have looked at this process is that failing public schools put a great deal of pressure, not only on the system, but also on communities. It puts pressure on families, and when families have an opportunity for an alternative such as a faith-based institution, they make the choice.

Also it's interesting to me as I have seen the choices made by those who are teachers in many of these faith-based institutions. As we were doing an analysis of the 40-some teachers that are teaching at the Allen Christian School, for instance, we discovered that 38 percent of those (teachers) at Allen Christian School have been there more than 18 years.

That's saying much when you consider that our salary scale is about two-thirds of that of a public school teacher. It means that the environment is, as I think Bill just said to us, an inviting environment, an encouraging environment, a supportive environment, a place where teachers want to be, and where teachers want to teach and where they do more than teach because, in most instances, they become extensions of the family in a much more meaningful way.

But the problem is that as I look at – I looked a few weeks ago at our finances and realized that the church actually subsidizes to the tune of about $1.5 to $1.9 million a year. That kind of money coming out of the budget of the church means that it is not doing some of those things that are required in its ministry. And only to the degree that we convince the leadership of the church that it is a part of our ministry are we able to continue to make that kind of funding.

When we started this process, we were giving the school $40,000 a month to maintain their utility costs and the mortgage on the building. What we have discovered, though, is the labor cost in these institutions is so great that we now have to search for partners to try to bring about a needful change in order for us to continue to educate in the way that we have in the past. And the way that we have in the past is the majority, over 90 percent, of our fourth-grade students are able to pass the statewide exams – which are not required of us – in reading, science, math, and social studies.

Good education helps to build good communities. It raises the standards of housing. It raises the standards of life expectations.

We've also found that at the eighth-grade level, Allen Christian School does better than any of the schools in the southeast Queens area in terms of its ability to have students that are test-ready, and not because we teach to the test, but because, I think, [we teach] all of the other values that are endemic in the overall educational process.

I do believe there is a place for the faith-based institutions. The problem, however, centers (on) an inability to have the resources, making it necessary to have a creative process by which we deliver the education, particularly when we consider ourselves responsible for creating an educational environment that is better than what is offered by the surrounding schools in the community.

For instance, in most of the schools in my neighborhood, they do not offer art. They do not have a band. They do not have the basic things that help to make for a whole well-rounded educational process. We believe that it is essential. Also, the freedom that we have taken to extend our days has meant a great deal in terms of having young people in reading readiness programs in the morning for an hour before the rest of the school day moves forward, has been phenomenal in assisting in getting them into a position where they are educationally ready for the rest of what we offer to them.

Also, those who are in the Catholic sector, the high schools in the New York community, particularly in the Queens community, are at our doors in October. Generally, the majority of those students who graduate from Allen Christian School go to high school at Catholic schools, because parents are used to paying tuition and because parents expect them to be in an environment where they continue with the same kind of learning trends.

And so St. Francis Prep, Molloy High School, Christ the King, and those schools that are part of that community wait for us because they say the young people coming out of Allen Christian School are, first of all, capable of passing the test, and when they get to the school they have the kind of discipline to continue to be competitive with those young people who are part of that educational environment.

And so we should not marginalize these schools. Rather, we should work hard to create new incentives so that these schools might be able to survive. Among those incentives might be tax incentives or tax credits for those parents who are not getting the quality of education from the public system that they ought and therefore have to make alternative choices.

We ought to also consider some bond financing or some support from the public sector, because we believe that we are doing a job for the public sector in preparing young people that are job-ready, young people that are college-ready, young people that institutions do not have to spend additional money on remedial programs to get them ready to be as competitive as they ought to be in the higher education community.

We also need to deal with the reality that, as we open these doors, the opportunities that are created for these young people put them at a major advantage in most instances, because colleges begin to look at our young people even before they finish the eighth grade to try to make determinations of curving them in a way where they get to the 12th grade, tracking them so that by the time they're in the 12th grade, they have followed them into their schools. A classic example was a young lady that just got invited to apply to Harvard University. And she was invited to apply not only because her grades were excellent at Allen, but her grades were also excellent at St. Francis Prep.

If we can do that on a wider scale, I believe that we can solve many of America's social problems. We can bring communities to positions where they are stronger than they have been in the past. We can indeed rebuild communities. I dare to believe that because Allen Church took over the responsibility, if you look at the statistics of where the community was before when it was considered a community that was lost, a community on the decline, it is now one of the upwardly mobile communities. And by the *New York Times'* statement it is a community that is third largest behind Decatur, Georgia and (Prince George's) County in Maryland just outside of D.C., with 65,000 or more African-Americans where the economics represent a community that is extremely strong.

Good education helps to build good communities, and those communities are the communities where people are not moving to the suburbs or looking for places to go where they can get a quality education. It also means raising the standards of housing. It raises the standards of life expectations, and it certainly raises the standards of individuals who dare to believe that someone in this generation will not be another statistic that will waste away in the jailhouse.

What we've discovered is that with that $5,400 per year tuition, grandmothers, uncles, cousins, everybody in the family is making the commitment that another child will not be lost and begins to make payments. So we get checks from all directions because people, if given the opportunity, will make investments in quality education.

Questions and Discussion

Karl Zinsmeister Wow. These were very meaty and interesting remarks for me and I hope for you. I don't think there's a strict principal out there who could fault these gentlemen on their discipline and their time management. They were all right on, so those of you who brought those heavy 16-inch rulers—I see some bulging in handbags—you can put those away. We are going to stay on schedule today.

We have time as a result of their discipline for about maybe eight to 10 minutes of questions before we move to the President's speech. I was very struck by what Reverend Flake said at the end. We all know that good schools tend to overlap with good neighborhoods, but I think we often think of that as kind of the order is, first, there's a good neighborhood and then there's a good school.

What Reverend Flake just told us is that the good school can become the source of the good neighborhood and actually help turn around the neighborhood and improve the rest of the culture and composition of the neighborhood. That's a really fascinating possibility. And one may again argue that even if you aren't motivated or moved at all by the religious aspect of these schools, you can understand the way they operate is in the common interest.

I wonder if any of the panelists want to elaborate on that possibility.

Reverend Flake Just one point. One of the things that you discover is that when you look at a community like Prince George's County, which is adjacent to Washington, D.C., people moved out of D.C. in large measure because they had expectations that in Prince George's County, where they were buying $300,000, $400,000 homes, they would not have to worry about how they were going to educate their children.

These are middle class people. They have means, predominantly African-Americans. There is no reason to assume that in that community they would not be able to properly educate their children. And yet many of people I know there are looking for alternatives simply because the community itself does not lend itself to the quality education they expected in the public system. So there are emerging schools as they're building these mega churches. Those mega churches have made decisions that not only do they build a church; they're also building schools to give support to a community where one would not expect that to be a necessity.

In our community it worked the other way because my survey showed that people were either moving out to Nassau County or moving up to Westchester County or moving back to the South. And so my theory was if we build a quality school, we will force the public schools around us to get better. And that has been done to a degree, not to the degree that I would like, but it has been done to such a degree that we've been able to raise the standards in housing quality to where people want to live. Of course we have built about 600 homes as well, and that makes a difference. So ours is a about a concept of an entire community, of which the school and the church are the center.

Audience Member A former governor of New York conducted a study years ago. I don't know if you saw that, but it was an astounding study. It was commissioned by the board of education in New York, and it said that more poor disadvantaged children attend parochial schools proportionately than public schools. That story never got out, and the whole report was glowing about the good job– they were doing.

I happened to run into Hugh Carey on Long Island one time, and I spoke with him about this about that report, and he said, "I never heard that anywhere." Is that known?

Reverend Flake Yeah. I think Joe may be able to speak to it, but my point on it would be if I look at the community of which I am a part, you cannot get a seat in a Catholic school in that neighborhood. And I say Catholic because that's the predominant alternative schools in terms of numbers. And when we were doing a program—Joe, we may have been doing that together – when we were looking at how we were going to place some students when they first entered through charters and vouchers and the like, we had some money because we had philanthropists. We didn't have the seats in the Catholic schools and in the faith-based institutions.

Viteritti You're right, though. That study did not get a lot of attention. I actually commissioned a subsequent study that focused on elementary schools, and again it showed that the Catholic schools were serving a very poor population, and they were doing a more effective job, particularly with poor populations. It was a very comprehensive study that I commissioned from the former head of evaluation in the New York City Public Schools, and it got very little attention. The press just ignored it.

Audience Member I believe it was Professor Glenn, and I want to talk about the research. You mentioned there's a lack of conspiracy to kill faith-based schools, and I would just like to present to the panel the option of what is happening in public schools teachers' union leadership that, in my opinion, may have actually been a conspiracy to thwart what's going on in the faith-based schools in the inner-city. That's kind of like the thousand-pound elephant in the middle of the room, but I'd like to throw it out there early.

Reverend Flake Well, the Blaine Amendment itself clearly is an indication that there is an antagonistic group. They put it in the charter school laws in New York for fear that many of our schools that are really living on the bubble financially were going to actually convert. So I would have to think that there is clearly an antagonistic mode as it relates to those who want to protect us by preserving what exists, which is not offering the quality education for the majority of those kids in those neighborhoods.

Glenn A number years ago the National Education Association decided they needed to hear a different voice, and so they asked me down to speak to the board at the national board meeting on the issue of parent choice of schools. And before my talk I was taken out to lunch by the member of the staff who at that point was responsible for opposing educational vouchers, a very nice African-American woman.

And we talked about our families and our children, and she mentioned that she had moved to Prince George's County to get away from the Washington schools, which did strike me as an exercise of parent choice. So I asked her how pleased she was with the Prince George's County schools. She said well, actually, she had put her children in Catholic schools. But she was in charge of opposing that possibility for poor parents, so I didn't say anything. She was a very nice lady, and she was paying for my lunch.

Audience Member This is for the second or third speaker perhaps, have you noticed any regional variation in the numbers that you described, and if so, why?

Jeynes Generally speaking, the areas of the country with the largest percentage of urban populations have the greatest reduction of the achievement gap. And so generally speaking, you're talking about the east and the Midwest and also the west. Less so in, say, the Rocky Mountain states or the south. So there is some degree of variation.

Audience Member I mean for cities.

Jeynes Not a lot of difference, although, generally, the areas of the country with larger cities—again, you're talking about the northeast—have the greatest reduction in the achievement gap. So the more urbanized the city, the greater reduction in the achievement gap.

I think a lot of what we shared today is that there's a lot of research available, but it really hasn't been publicized to the degree that it should be. And I think it's important that the news get out that the achievement gap is reduced and that the people who benefit the most by private religious schools are children of color and those of low socioeconomic status, particularly in the larger cities such as New York, Los Angeles, Chicago, and Detroit, these areas.

SPEECH BY PRESIDENT GEORGE W. BUSH

Aysia Mayo-Gray

Hello. My name is Aysia Mayo-Gray. I'm an eighth-grader at St. Ann's Academy in Washington, D.C. I'm a native Washingtonian and the oldest of three children. I have attended private school since kindergarten. I will be attending Elizabeth Seton Catholic High School in the fall.

I like St. Ann's because I feel as if it's my second home. Not only have I bonded with my classmates and teachers, but also other students in the lower grades. My favorite subject is language arts, followed by history. This year my class performed the Shakespeare play, "Titus Andronicus," at the Ford Theater and won several awards. This was a great experience for all of us.

At St. Ann's I'm known as Aysia and not just a student who attends the school. The teachers have well prepared me for the future and have given me the skills to meet the challenges to come.

At this time it's my honor and privilege to introduce to you the President of the United States, George W. Bush.

In: Disadvantaged Students and Crisis in…
Editor: Thomas G. Wilson

ISBN: 978-1-60741-535-0

Chapter 3

THE PRESIDENT

The White House Domestic Policy Council

Thank you, all. Aysia, thanks for the introduction—you did a fabulous job. I'm told that you're a very hard worker who loves school, and it's clear you always wear a smile. She's a member of her school's Student Advisory Group, has performed in plays ranging from Shakespeare to "The Lion King," (and) writes short stories. And as you just heard her explain, she loves all language arts. Well, that's good—some people say I'm pretty artful with language, as well.

It is clear she has a promising future because of the education she is receiving at Saint Ann's. Unfortunately, thousands of other children like her are missing out on these opportunities because America's inner-city faith-based schools are closing at an alarming rate. And so that's why we've convened this summit: to discuss how we can extend lifelines of learning to all America's children. And I want to thank you for coming.

I take this summit seriously. Obviously you do, as well. My Administration looks forward to working with you. This is a national objective, to make sure every child gets a good education. And I really appreciate you coming.

America's inner-city faith-based schools are closing at an alarming rate. And so that's why we've convened this summit: to discuss how we can extend lifelines of learning to all America's children.

I want to thank my friend and Secretary of Education, Margaret Spellings, for joining with us today. I thank the Acting Secretary of HUD, Roy Bernardi.

Archbishop Wuerl, thank you very much, sir, for being here. We were just talking about what a glorious week it was to welcome His Holiness to America. It was an extraordinary moment for all who were directly involved, and I think an extraordinary moment for all of America. I got to know Archbishop Wuerl in Pittsburgh. I hope I conveyed to him my sense that providing a sound education for every child is one of the really important challenges for America. I happen to believe it is one of the greatest civil rights challenges. I am fully aware that in inner-city America some children are getting a good education, but a lot are consigned to inadequate schools.

And I believe helping these children should be a priority of the nation. It's certainly a priority to me. I married a teacher who has worked in inner-city schools; I helped raise one, as well. And helping inner-city children receive the education they deserve is so important as we head into the 21st century to make sure every child has got the skills necessary to succeed. That's what a hopeful country is all about.

Over the past seven years we have worked to strengthen the public school system. In other words, we haven't given up on public schools; quite the contrary, we've tried to help them succeed by passing the No Child Left Behind Act. In some circles it's controversial. I don't think it should be controversial, however, to demand high standards for every child. I don't think it should be controversial to insist upon accountability to see if those children are meeting those standards. And I don't think it should be viewed as controversial to say to a public school, if children are falling behind, here are supplementary services to help that individual child catch up.

As a result of accountability measures, I can now say that eighth-graders set a record high for math scores. In other words, in order to be able to say that, you have to measure in the first place. When I was governor of Texas, I didn't like a system where we just simply guessed "Do you think the child is learning?" "I don't know, maybe, maybe not." That's unacceptable, particularly when a child's life is at stake.

We've learned that scores for minority and poor students are reaching all-time highs in a number of areas... The problem is that while the No Child Left Behind Act is helping to turn around many struggling schools, there are still children trapped in schools that will not teach and will not change.

We've learned that scores for minority and poor students are reaching all-time highs in a number of areas. And that's great. As a matter of fact, there's an achievement gap in America that is unacceptable. The good news is it's beginning to narrow. The problem is that while the No Child Left Behind Act is helping to turn around many struggling schools, there are still children trapped in schools that will not teach and will not change.

Today nearly one-half of children in America's major urban school districts do not graduate on time—one-half of our children in major urban school districts do not get out of school on time. In Detroit, one student in four makes it out of the public school system with a diploma. When schools like these fail our inner-city children it is unfair, it's unacceptable, and it is unsustainable for our country.

And so there are a variety of solutions. One is to work hard to improve the public school system, but also another solution is to recognize that there is a bright future for a lot of children found in faith-based schools.

The faith-based school tradition is not a 21st-century phenomenon. A Quaker school opened in Philadelphia in 1689. A Jewish day school opened in New York more than 40 years before the American Revolution. During the 19th century, Catholic schools in our biggest cities welcomed children of poor, European immigrants. Can you imagine what it's like to be an immigrant coming to America, cannot hardly speak the language, and find great solace in two institutions – one, church; and two, schools? And generations of Americans have been lifted up. Generations of the newly arrived have been able to have hopeful futures because of our faith-based schools. It's a fact. It's a part of our history. Frankly, it's a glorious part of our history.

Today, in our poorest communities, religious schools continue to provide important services. And as they carry out their historic mission of training children in faith, these schools increasingly serve children that don't share their religious tradition. That's important for people to know, that there's a lot of students who, for example, may not be Catholic, who go to the schools and get a great education. That's what we ought to be focused on: how to get people a great education.

Generations of the newly arrived have been able to have hopeful futures because of our faith-based schools. It's a fact. It's a part of our history. Frankly, it's a glorious part of our history.

In neighborhoods where some people say children simply cannot learn, the faith-based schools are proving the naysayers wrong. These schools provide a good, solid academic foundation for children. They also help children understand the importance of discipline and character.

Yet for all the successes, America's inner-city faith-based schools are facing a crisis. And I use the word "crisis" for this reason: Between 2000 and 2006, nearly 1,200 faith-based schools closed in America's inner cities. It's affected nearly 400,000 students. They're places of learning where people are getting a good education and they're beginning to close, to the extent that 1,200 of them have closed. The impact of school closings extends far beyond the children that are having to leave these classrooms. The closings place an added burden on inner-city public schools that are struggling. And these school closings impoverish our country by really denying...future... children a critical source of learning not only about how to read and write, but also about social justice.

We have an interest in the health of these institutions. One of the reasons I've come is to highlight this problem and say to our country: We have an interest in the health of these centers of excellence. It's in the country's interest to get beyond the debate of public/private, to recognize this is a critical national asset that provides a critical part of our nation's fabric in making sure we are a hopeful place.

And so I want to spend a little time talking about what can be done to help preserve these schools and provide, more importantly, a hopeful future. And that's what you're going to do after I leave, as well.

We have an interest in the health of these institutions... these centers of excellence. It's in the country's interest to get beyond the debate of public-private, to recognize this is a critical national asset that provides a critical part of our nation's fabric.

First, ensuring that faith-based schools can continue to serve inner-city children requires a commitment from the Federal government. Federal funds support faith-based organizations that serve Americans in need. We got beyond the social service debate by saying that it's okay to use taxpayers' money to provide help for those who hurt. My whole theory of life was we ought to be asking about results, not necessarily process. When you focus on process you can find all sorts of reasons not to move forward. If you say focus on results, it then provides an outlet for options other than State-sponsored programs—which is okay.

What I'm telling you is that we are using taxpayers' money to empower faith-based organizations to help meet critical needs throughout the country—critical needs such as helping a child whose parents may be in prison understand there's hope; a critical need is helping a prisoner recently released realize there's a hopeful tomorrow; a critical need is to help somebody whip drugs and alcohol so they can live a hopeful life. And we do that in the social services.

We also provide federal funding support for institutions of higher learning. We are using taxpayers' money to enable somebody to go to a private university, a religious university. It's a long tradition of the United States of America.

So my attitude is if we are doing this, if this is a precedent, why don't we use the same philosophy to provide federal funds to help inner-city families find greater choices in educating their children?

There is a precedent for this called the D.C. Choice Incentive Act. And we've got some advocates here for the D.C. Choice Incentive Act—I know, I've worked with them. The law created Washington's Opportunity Scholarship Program, which has helped more than 2,600 of the poorest children in our nation's capital find new hope at a faith-based or other nonpublic school. In other words, one way to address the closings of schools is to empower parents to be able to send their children to those schools before they close.

This is a successful program, I think it's safe to say. One way to judge whether it's successful is to look at the demand for the scholarship relative to the supplies of the scholarships. There are a lot of people who want their children to be able to take advantage of this program. As a matter of fact, demand clearly outstrips supply—which says to me we ought to expand the program and not kill the program.

So we'll continue to work with Congress to not only reauthorize the program as it exists, but hopefully also expand it.

I also proposed an idea that I really hope Congress takes seriously, and that is Pell Grants for Kids. This would be a $300 million initiative that would help as many as 75,000 low-income children that are now enrolled in troubled public schools to be able to go to a school of the parents' choice. What's very important to make sure that an accountability system works is there's actual consequences and outlets.

And one of the outlets would be if you're in a public school that won't teach and won't change and you qualify, here's a scholarship for you to be able to have an additional opportunity. And to me this is a good way to help strengthen the schools that I was talking about that we are losing. One way to make sure you don't lose schools is you have people that are able to afford the education—sustain the cash flow of these valuable American assets.

I want to remind our citizens Pell Grants have helped low-income young adults pursue the dream of a college education. And it is time to apply the same spirit to liberate poor children trapped in public schools that aren't meeting expectations.

State and local governments can help. Today, more than 30 State constitutions include so-called Blaine Amendments, which prohibit public support of religious schools. These amendments have their roots in 19th century anti-Catholic bigotry, and today the legacy of discrimination continues to harm low-income students of many faiths and many backgrounds. And so State lawmakers, if they're concerned about quality education for children, and if they're concerned about these schools closing, ought to remove the Blaine Amendments.

I want to remind our citizens Pell Grants have helped low-income young adults pursue the dream of a college education. And it is time to apply the same spirit to liberate poor children trapped in public schools that aren't meeting expectations.

There are other things State and local governments can do. I would call people's attention to the Pennsylvania Educational Improvement Tax Credit, PEITC, which allows businesses to meet State tax obligations by supporting pre-K through 12 scholarships for low-income students. It's an innovative way to use the tax code to meet a national—in this case, State—objective. The scholarships then allow children to attend the school of their choice, including religious schools. Since 2001, these tax credits have yielded more than $300 million to help Pennsylvania families. It's an innovative use of the tax code to meet social objectives. All 12 high schools in the Pittsburgh district have seen increased enrollments each year the program has been in place. That's positive.

And so I would call upon State leaders to listen to what comes out of this conference and to think of innovative ways to advance education for all children. Faith-based schools can continue to serve inner-city children; to see that that happens requires a commitment from the business community. It's in corporate America's interest that our children get a good education, starting in pre-K through 12th grade.

In Chicago a group of Jesuit priests found an innovative way to finance children's education called Cristo Rey, and they convinced Chicago's businesses to become involved. It's interesting that the Jesuits took the initiative. I would hope that corporate America would also take initiative. But four days of the week the children go to class and then on the fifth they report for work at some of Chicago's most prestigious firms.

The businesses get energetic, reliable workers for high-turnover jobs. The students get a top-notch education plus real work experience. They feel a sense of pride when they leave some of the city's most dangerous neighborhoods for the city's tallest skyscrapers. It's a program that is working, and many of the students take that same sense of pride and accomplishment to higher education.

In neighborhoods where some people say children simply cannot learn, the faith-based schools are proving the naysayers wrong. These schools provide a good, solid academic foundation for children. They also help children understand the importance of discipline and character.

It's interesting to note that Cristo Rey is now involved in 19 cities. In other words, good ideas can take hold. The job of this conference is to provide a kind of go-by for people who share a sense of concern about our nation's future. And hopefully from this summit good ideas will be spawning other good ideas—at the Federal level and the State and local level, at the corporate level and then of course at the citizen level.

Citizens, we are a compassionate nation. What I see is America at its very best, which (are) these millions of acts of kindness and generosity that take place, and it doesn't require a government law. Sometimes it takes a little higher authority than government to inspire people to acts of kindness and mercy. But it happens all the time in America. It truly does. One-third of Americans who volunteer do so through religious organizations. Many of them happen to be faith-based schools, by the way. When you hear about an America that volunteers, (know that) many of the volunteers are at faith-based schools.

I was struck by an interesting story that came out of Memphis, Tennessee. Ten years ago private donors gave approximately $15 million to the church in Memphis to help revive Catholic schools in the city's poorest neighborhoods. Assets exist; they're worried about them going away; so rather than just watch schools close, somebody did something about it by putting up $15 million. With the seed money, the diocese launched the Jubilee Schools initiative and reopened Catholic schools that had been shuttered, actually in some cases, for decades. Today, 10 Jubilee schools serve more than 1,400 students. Eighty-one percent of these children are not Catholic; nearly 96 percent live at or below the poverty level.

With the help from Jubilee scholarship donors, tuition becomes whatever the family can afford. And the schools happen to be working, as well, which is really important. And the reason I can tell you (that) is because test scores are up, they're not afraid to measure. You've got to be a little worried in our society when somebody says, "I don't think I want to measure." That's like saying, "I don't want to be held to account." The problem with that line of reasoning is that when you're dealing with our children, it's unacceptable. Of course you should be held to account. We ought to praise those who achieve excellence, and call upon those who don't to change so they can achieve excellence.

And so this school system is willing to measure, and it has been a great joy for the people of Memphis to watch excellence spread. And I want to thank those who have put forth the money and call on all citizens to find ways they can contribute with their hearts to help educational entrepreneurs succeed. (This) is really what we are talking about, is it not? Innovation, they're willing to challenge the status quo if it's not working. I call it educational entrepreneurship, so I'd consider (you) entrepreneurs, social entrepreneurs.

Faith-based schools can continue to serve inner-city children and sometimes they can get a good boost from higher education. When I was governor of Texas, I tried to get our higher education institutions to understand that rather than becoming a source of remediation, they ought to be a source of added value. And one way to do so is to help these schools early on, to make sure that children don't slip behind in the basics.

The impact of school closings extends far beyond the children that are leaving these classrooms. The closings place an added burden on inner-city public schools that are struggling. And these school closings impoverish our country by denying future children a critical source of learning.

I was impressed by Notre Dame's Alliance for Catholic Education, known as ACE, which prepares college graduates to work as teachers in under-served Catholic schools. It's an interesting way to participate in making sure the Catholic schools and the faith-based schools stay strong, and that is to educate teachers—actually go in the classrooms to make sure that there's adequate instruction available. The people at Notre Dame commit to teach for two years as they earn their master's degree in education. And it turns out that when you get a taste for being a teacher, you tend to stay. And so today there are about 650 ACE teachers and graduates who work at Catholic schools across the country.

I like the idea of these higher education institutions saying, "Here's what I can contribute to making sure that elementary school and junior high school and high school education has high standards and excellence." And one way to do it is to support our faith-based schools all across the country.

And so that's what I've come to talk to you about. These are levels of society that ought to all be involved, and hopefully out of this meeting, there's concrete action. We didn't ask you to come to Washington just to opine; we came and asked you to Washington to set good ideas out there for others to go by, because there's a lot of people in our country who share the same concern you share—people understand what we are talking about here. This is pretty practical stuff. These are down-to-earth ideas on how to solve some of our nation's critical problems.

Let me end with a story here about Yadira Vieyra. Yadira says she goes to Georgetown University ... I was asking if Yadira was going to be here so I could ask her to stand here in a minute, and a fellow told me she's a little worried about missing class. So whoever Yadira's teacher is, please blame it on me, not her.

She was born in Mexico—Mexicana. And they moved to Chicago, probably to try to realize a better life—I'm confident, to try to realize a better life. Mom and dad had a dream to give their family hope. There's no more hopeful place in the world, by the way, than the United States of America. We should not be surprised when people come to America for a hopeful life. That's what America has been and should be.

And then we should not be surprised when the parents hope that their children get a great education, because there's nothing more hopeful for a parent than to know their child is receiving a good education. Well, that's what Yadira's folks wanted for her. So when the time came for her to go to high school, they wanted something better than a low-performing high school. One of the interesting things about the accountability system: a lot of people think that their child goes to the finest school ever, until the results get posted.

The whole purpose, by the way, is not to embarrass anybody; it's not to scold anybody. The whole purpose is to achieve excellence for every person. And so Yadira's parents, I'm sure, took a look at the school system and said there's a better way. And so she went to Cristo Rey, the program I just described to you. And she was challenged by the school's rigorous academics.

If you set low standards, guess what you're going to get? Low results. If you believe in every child's worth and every child can learn, it's important to set high standards and challenge the children, and that's what happened in the school she went to. She was inspired by great teachers. She said she was motivated by the school's amazing job program. And she is now at Georgetown University, one of the great universities in America. And guess what she wants to do when she leaves Georgetown? She wants to enroll in Notre Dame's ACE program. Yadira, thanks for coming.

You either just got an A or an F. Either case, we are glad you're here and I love your example. And the reason why it's important to have examples is so that we get beyond the rhetoric and realize that we are dealing with the human potential. No telling what Yadira's going to be in life, but one thing is for certain: it's going to be a productive citizen, and America will be better for it. And so we are glad you're here. Thank you for your spirit. Tell your parents, thank you.

And so let me close with what happened at National Stadium with (the) Holy Father. When he celebrated mass there, one of the objects he blessed at the end of the mass was the new cornerstone of the Pope John Paul the Great High School in Arlington, Virginia. Is that not interesting? I'm sure there (were) a lot of demands on His Holy Father, but he took time to bless the cornerstone of a school.

And my hope is that we are laying cornerstones for new schools here or revived schools; that we take the spirit of the Holy Father and extend it throughout the country and work for excellence for every child; to set high standards, and when we find centers of excellence, not (let) them go away, but to think of policy that will enable them to not only exist, not only survive, but also to thrive. It's in our nation's interest. It's an important summit for America.

I thank you for bringing your talents, your energies and your efforts. I thank you for caring deeply about our young. And I thank you for being a part of what I believe is a necessary strategy to make sure America continues to be a hopeful place for all. God bless you. Thank you, all.

In: Disadvantaged Students and Crisis in…
Editor: Thomas G. Wilson

ISBN: 978-1-60741-535-0

Chapter 4

PANEL II: PRACTICAL REALITIES ON THE GROUND

The White House Domestic Policy Council

JAY HEIN

I think it's fair to say we could not have gotten off to a better start. We had an expert panel. Karl Zinsmeister from our first panel gave us expert opinions about the issues, and we received such inspiration from The President who says that he cares about this issue, and Americans should care about this issue. Then he gives us a call to action that engages every sector of society. This is good news. This is good news. They're paying attention to this issue.

And this panel will deliver the next step in the journey. They'll give you a voice from movement leaders and from the streets, the voice of the end user, in many respects, of this system. And we are going to begin to move forward to this multi-sector solution that the President asked us to pursue.

First I'd like to give you just a few quick motivations of why I'm so pleased to be in your company before I introduce these four very fine leaders. My name is Jay Hein. I direct the White House Office of Faith-based and Community Initiatives. I am the son of two Wisconsin public educators. My father was a guidance counselor at our high school, and my mother was a kindergarten teacher on an Indian reservation. And they taught me the value of public education, education generally, and I was a product of public education, and I'm grateful, therefore, for President Bush's leadership to reform American public schools and Secretary Spellings' commitment to the same.

I am also the father of two sons, one who goes to a faith-based private school and one who goes to a public school. I am grateful for both of those institutions, and I am grateful that I had a choice. We picked the right school for two very different boys. I don't know how that happens. You can grow them up in the same home, and they have different needs. And I am painfully aware of what we talked about today, that not every parent has that choice, so we need to expand that choice.

Private faith has public value, distinctive public value.

I was, third, a board member of an inner-city classical education school in Indianapolis, Indiana, before I joined my current post. And now I'm director of faith-based initiatives, so I understand that private faith has public value, distinctive public value. And I'm so proud to work for a President who reminds us of that and who tells me every day to do everything I can and our initiative can to support you in those institutions, which are very valuable.

You're very valuable public servants, and I thank you for your service. I will now introduce each of our speakers in the order in which they will address you. And our first speaker is Phylicia Lyons, who is a very proud graduate of Reverend Floyd Flake's academic institution that he has told us about, the Allen Christian School. She is founder, president, and CEO of School Choice Illinois, which advocates for private educational opportunities for low-income children in her State. You're about to be very impressed by her.

She went on from her New York education to attend two very prestigious college and post-college institutions and now is deploying her talent on behalf of other students like herself, because she wants to extend the same opportunities to Chicago's youth that she enjoyed, thanks to the incredible sacrifice of her parents and particularly her mother after her father's passing, which she'll tell you about. She's surely an example, and we are thrilled to have her. She will lead off here.

Our next panelist is the Reverend Joseph O'Keefe, who is dean of the Lynch School of Education of Boston College. Reverend O'Keefe is training the next generation of leaders, the administrators and teachers at Catholic institutions. He's also an esteemed academic, not of broad theory but of practical applications of education in communities, and so he has become a leading thinker and writer on the State of play that we are talking about today. So he is a scholar practitioner, and we are so honored to have him in our company.

Third we will hear from Vernard Gant, who is director of Urban School Services at the Association of Christian Schools International. Like Phylicia Lyons, Dr. Gant benefitted from high-quality inner-city education in a distressed environment, and he is a terrific product of such an education. And he too wants to extend that blessing to others. He has dedicated 30 years of his professional life to improving the life outcome of urban children, for the past 20 years in particular advancing urban education models.

So we are honored to have you and eager to hear what you have to say. And then the anchor of this fine panel is Virginia Walden-Ford, who happens to be the one whom the President hugged right up here. She is the executive director of D.C. Parents for Choice and was the little engine that could behind that effort, and we are so in her debt.

I should just say very quickly that this panel is pretty excited that the President of the United States was their opening act. It's really special, and they asked me if they could do the rope line after the panel gets done.

I said, "No, we are going to have to move to the next panel." But Virginia is going to remind you of the power of the consumer's voice and what she's done to mobilize the parents here in Washington, D.C., which is a replicable strategy, and it is an unmatched strategy because when we can hear from parents themselves and hear it forcefully, systems change. Mountains move, and that's what happened here in Washington, D.C.

But she'll also tell you that not all parents are naturally inclined. They don't know that they have the right to a choice, and they oftentimes are defeated by their circumstances. It takes equipping and serving these parents, just as it does us to gather in the movement that we are enjoying each other's company and events today. So without further ado, I invite our first speaker to the podium.

Phylicia Lyons

I'm excited after that first panel and hearing from the President. I'm just ready to get out there and go into Chicago and take to the streets and just take the world by storm.

I know many of you are working out in the field. It's really been an inspiration for us to really start to move forward. So I just want to say it's a pleasure to stand before you to share my story of hope and promise and to serve on this distinguished panel. And I remember the words of Mrs. Anderson. She was my elementary school teacher, and her words resound in my ears. She said, "Oh, Phylicia, she's going to become a teacher." I can hear her say those words over and over again. "Oh she's too smart for you silly boys," she used to say to the boys who used to pick on me at school.

And since those days I have done all that I can to avoid teaching. And today I'm the founder and CEO, president of School Choice Illinois, an independent nonprofit organization that advocates for expanded kindergarten through 12th-grade education throughout the State of Illinois.

I'm living proof of the importance of faith-based schools and quality school options. Without the unique experience and education offered to me by my faith-based school, I can say without a doubt, I would have become yet another statistic.

Well, I have to say that my elementary school teacher was not far off the mark. She, like many other teachers of mine, had this notion that we were going to become more than we could even imagine. And I'd like to think she was dead on about those silly boys, present company excluded of course.

But I'm living proof of the importance of faith-based schools and quality school options. Without the unique experience and education offered to me by my faith-based school, I can say without a doubt, I would have become yet another statistic. You see, I was raised by a young widowed mother in southeast Queens, New York in the 1980s. However, 1983 has two significant meanings for me. Firstly, it marks the year America was declared a nation at risk, where the standards of mediocrity were confirmed as real and pervasive in our public education system while private education really didn't face those academic challenges.

Secondly, 1983 was the year that my sister and I, ages three and five, respectively, enrolled in Allen Christian School, a faith-based school founded by Reverend Dr. Floyd H. Flake, a former U.S. congressman. On this 25th year anniversary, we still face an educational crisis, and the future of many of our children hang in the balance. In fact, according to the most recent statistics, only 17 percent of Latinos and 11 percent of black public high school graduates in Illinois graduate college-ready.

Additionally, we have a crisis of a different front. Most of our schools or many of our schools that historically provided some of the nation's neediest and most vulnerable children a quality education and vigorous education are on the decline. The record numbers show that faith-based schools have closed across America. From the previous statistics, they show that in Chicago, 66 of our Catholic schools have closed, and that's actually the largest number across the nation.

My faith-based school offered me more than just a comprehensive, high-quality education. We had many teachers like Mrs. Anderson who believed that I was full of hope and promise. Our teachers and administrators went above and beyond their call of duty to prepare students like myself for lifelong learning. My faith-based school offered me hope, encouragement, support, direction, purpose, refuge, and safety during my most formative years. The school was a beacon of light for our community. It was a ray of hope for a previously neglected neighborhood and a powerhouse of love, support and peace.

Faith teaching as well was such a critical element in my academic life. I learned a sense of moral discipline, self-worth and community obligation. As faith-based schools grow extinct across America, can we confidently say that the remaining schools are currently equipped to meet the educational and emotional needs of all children? Well, based on my professional and personal experiences, I can emphatically say no.

It was my faith-based elementary school experience that prepared me to excel at Catholic high school, to earn a Bachelor of Arts degree from the University of Virginia, to earn a master of public policy degree from the Irving B. Harris Graduate School of Public Policy Studies at the University of Chicago—it's a long name. I've also lived, worked, and studied in Western Europe and Central America. I've also contributed to the fields of public policy, telecommunications, finance, technology research, consulting, and international relations.

Instead of lamenting the disappearance of faith-based schools across America, let us take this as an opportunity to revitalize our schools with resources, financial support, and new public policies. By doing so, we will bring hope and a chance for success for all of our nation's children.

Our Christian school was my launching pad, and without it I would not have had the educational and emotional support I needed to succeed in life at my early age. Today, because of those experiences, I am committed to fighting for equal access to quality K–12 public and private schools. I wholeheartedly believe that all children are full of hope and promise. Where they're languishing in ill-performing or ill-equipped or poor-performing schools, children need that chance to attend quality schools that will help them build a foundation for their future success in the same way it prepared me.

Instead of lamenting the disappearance of faith-based schools across America, let us take this as an opportunity to revitalize our schools with resources, financial support, and new public policies. By doing so, we will bring hope and a chance for success for all of our nation's children. What greater legacy can I leave? What greater legacy could you leave than to have our children say that we worked really hard to make equal educational opportunities a reality?

And for the child who cannot vote, for the child who cannot write a check to a political campaign or a special interest membership organization, for the child whose parents are just working to make sure there's food on the table or to keep the lights on, for the child who's being raised by a single parent, we must stand up. We must speak up.

It's our turn to act on their behalf. I see these children. I see America's children as chief executive officers of billion-dollar companies, as innovators of new medical technologies, as scientists, attorneys, and teachers. I too see our children negotiating peace treaties and even as future presidential hopefuls. When you see what I see, no cost is too high, no battle too hard, nor a journey too long for the pursuit of access to quality education for all.

Whether it's tuition tax credits, vouchers, tax-supported scholarships, competitive teacher salaries, or a combination of all these different public policies befitting each State or city, today is the day we must say, first, thank you to the education pioneers. And then we must say yes to the work ahead of us, and we must say yes to giving every child a chance. Every one of our nation's children deserves a chance. I believe that. They all deserve a chance. I sure did. Thank you.

REVEREND JOSEPH O'KEEFE

Good morning. I'm delighted to continue this conversation. I want to talk about Catholic schools in the inner-city today, and certainly I think we all see the need for innovation, for new solutions, because we've seen the sad result of inertia. When that does not happen, these inner-city schools perish. Necessity is the mother of invention, and I think we are at a great moment of opportunity.

Now, first of all, we have to say this. This is a legacy that is certainly worth saving. We heard about the Blaine Amendment. We heard about the origins of many of these urban Catholic schools that were, as Bishop McQuaid said, protective fortresses for young Catholic children. The Catholic population from these urban centers has experienced unprecedented upward mobility by any number of socioeconomic indicators and also an outward mobility away from those geographic neighborhoods to the suburbs and exurbs and also away from the Northeast and the Midwest to the growth of the South and the West.

Replacing them were immigrants and African-Americans from the South to our urban centers. And one of things that became evident for those schools that did stay open, they were remarkably effective in serving the new population, just as they were effective in serving the old population. Now, through the '80s there were a large number of closings and into the '90s. And I looked at those closings, the pattern of closings in the mid-'90s and then decided someone has to look at those who stayed open. What do we know about these inner-city schools?

High expectations, a demanding curriculum for everyone, a belief that every child can succeed. These are the important hallmarks of these schools.

So we decided to do a survey of inner-city schools to collect baseline data about these institutions. And nothing is more helpful, I think, in national planning than empirical data about what's happening on the ground. And you can see the kind of issues that we looked at in our study that was done in 2000–01 of 384 Catholic inner-city schools around the country.

Now, sadly—and I'll get back to this—25 percent of those schools are now closed. And we are embarking on a study to look at where these schools closed, but especially this summer and into next year we'll be doing a study at Boston College about how schools stayed open and beat the odds, because we certainly need to learn from one another.

Let me talk about these inner-city schools in three ways. I want to talk first about students, then about staffing, and then about structure. In regard to students, I think the most important issues that I want to raise are that these schools were easy to get into and difficult to get thrown out of. And very often what we hear is the impact of faith-based schools is not due to the schools themselves but rather is due to the self-selection by parents whose children are bound for success anyway, a kind of elitism within the inner-city only serving those, creaming the top if you will.

So certainly I think we need look at the schools and to say that we serve the same population as the public schools, in the Catholic schools especially. I think it's important to mention that 34 percent of my sample students were not Catholic, and I would imagine it will increase. But also no one had looked at who the non-Catholics are: by and large African-American Protestants. And I think there's an important ecumenical dimension to these schools that we need to pay close attention to.

As I said, open admission and high retention. It's not an elite group. However the most important dimension is—for all of them – very high aspiration. High aspirations come from high expectations, and I think that is a hallmark of all the schools that we are talking about today. Certainly Tony Bryk and others have mentioned this. High expectations, a demanding curriculum for everyone, a belief that every child can succeed: (these are the) important hallmarks of these schools.

Let me talk to you a little bit about staffing. And we have some significant challenges because when we look at teacher recruitment and retention, by and large it is a picture of a revolving door of younger teachers and older teachers who struggle, given the financial difficulties, the low salaries, the insufficient health care plans, the insufficient retirement plans.

And so, as a result, what we need to do is really look at adequate compensation, certainly for teachers across the country in all sectors, but especially in these faith-based schools. We had mentioned certainly the sisters and the brothers and the religious. You know, the Catholic community for years resourced its schools through human beings, lifelong volunteers called sisters, women religious who've done a remarkable job in lifting up the Catholic population and others who work in our schools.

And certainly when we look at the demographics that we saw at the outset today, that is a pool of volunteers that no longer exists in significant numbers. And for those that do like myself as a Jesuit, I need to earn a full salary because I have a lot of older brothers that I need to take care of. That's the demographic of religious life. When we look at the principals, for example, of these schools, 40 percent of them are women religious, generally they're in their 60s with a high level of education, lots of experience, but who worked for a stipend. There are real staffing challenges.

One of the other notable features was the lack of professionals other than teachers and administrators within these schools. Now, I'm not for bloating up a bureaucracy, but I think it is important that we look at the diverse needs of these schools and seek the kind of professional care very often needed. Now some of that was filled—the importance of volunteerism—and the President talked about volunteerism and how that is a hallmark of these schools. However, I think we need to do that in a more systematic way.

Let us take a look at the structure of these schools. Now, by and large (it is) very traditional. You know, it's no longer a sister with 60 students, but much of it remains the same, and there's a real advantage that these schools have been immune from kind of the fad *de jour* stuff that happens in education. However, there have been some significant changes. First, the growth of the early childhood sector, and we know that we need to start with very young children if they are to be bound for education success.

We know that given the dynamics of family, the traditional school day, the traditional school year doesn't work anymore. Extended time—we know we have real challenges in faith-based schools often driven by budgets (and) a digital divide. We know that to prepare leaders for the mid-21st century—which is our vocation and call—will require a technological savvy that often we haven't been able to provide.

One of the emerging features I think that's important, even if we make it through our operating budgets, half the schools that I surveyed were built before 1926. We have enormous capital expenses that loom ahead of us even if we make it through our operating budget.

Finally, a lot of the issues that I mention in here—the diverse needs of kids, the various issues—the schools that succeed are the schools that learn how to collaborate. It cannot be the school by itself. A school must collaborate with a variety of community agencies to make the school functional and viable.

Now sadly, since this study was done, elementary school enrollment in Catholic schools has declined by 24.7 percent in the 12 urban dioceses, clearly reflective also of my sample (see Figure 9). And you can see the number of children who don't have the opportunities they should have. It is a crisis, but there are signs of hope. Certainly the NativityMiguel and Cristo Rey—and we'll be hearing about that from B.J. Cassin later—and also the kinds of restructuring.

Again, it's "innovate or perish;" (requiring) the decoupling often of schools and parishes that can no longer support the school and finding new arrangements that are much more engaging of the entire Catholic community and the entire community beyond the church itself; (or) looking at consortium arrangements that are so crucial; (or) looking at collaboration with health care providers and with social service providers; (or) collaborating with public schools. One of the most important things we need to do is to stress time and time again that we are all committed to children in our inner cities no matter what kind of school they're in, and they have to have faith-based schools as an alternative.

And, finally, you know, I often say one of the great strengths of faith-based schools is their autonomy. The great weakness of faith-based schools is their autonomy. (There's) too much reinvention of the wheel. We need to learn how to replicate. And certainly trying to do that, in 2003, 2006, and 2008, Boston College with the National Catholic Educational Association is bringing together the best programs in the country that serve inner-city kids, what we call our endangered species within the Catholic church.

This too is looking at design for success, new configurations of Catholic schools that offer tremendous hope. So replication is important, and certainly, as the President said, that's much of what we are doing here today.

One of the most important things we need to do is to stress time and time again that we are all committed to children in our inner cities no matter what kind of school they're in, and they have to have faith-based schools as an alternative.

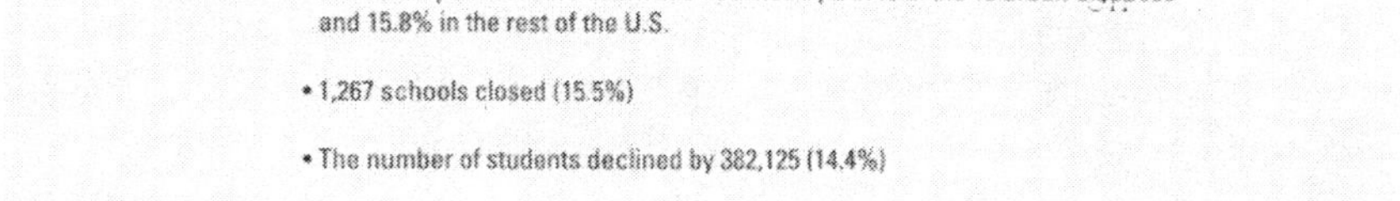

Reverend Joseph O'Keefe, "White House Summit on Inner-City Children and Faith Based Schools," (presentation, The White House, Washington, D.C., April 24, 2008).

Figure 9. Between 2000 and 2008...

Finally—how to move forward? It's all about innovation, entrepreneurial leadership, and bold, courageous decisions. And, you know, sometimes in the Catholic community we need to look back to our founders and at other faith-based communities too, in early days that were not the heydays of the '60s. But these were pioneers. And often they embarked upon ventures that never worked, but they kept going, and they kept trying, and they kept courage with very few people, with very few resources, but they were fueled by a mission that they would not surrender, and we need to do the same thing.

We need to collaborate, public sector, private sector. Thank God one of the things Catholic universities are starting to do is work together. There's a wake-up call for us to serve faith-based schools, and we are doing that together. Sustained philanthropy certainly is crucial for us. You know, it used to be bake sales and bingo. Now it's estate planning and capital campaigns. There has to be much more sophistication for sustained philanthropy.

And then, finally, we need to imagine a new public support for faith-based schools. Professor Glenn certainly outlined for us our situation within the world, just completed a work last year looking at 34 countries around the world that have Catholic schools. There are other ways to do this than we have done traditionally, and the days to have Blaine amendments should be in the past. We have an exciting future, and let us work together.

Vernard Gant

Good morning. Eight years ago this month, I had the high honor to be hired by the Association of Christian Schools International to start and give leadership to a department of urban school services that would focus upon those schools throughout our membership that target and serve children living in our urban centers, the underresourced child, the minority child, that child who was socially, academically at risk. These schools that had started as centers of hope to say to the children in a very evangelistic way, in its truest sense opening their doors and saying, "Whosoever will may come" and providing these children with a quality education.

And we spell quality A-B-C. An education that is academically excellent, Bible-based, and character-shaped. These schools that were offering to these parents the kind of hope that perhaps the parents themselves had not realized. And my wife and I had the opportunity to start two such schools in Birmingham where we were living at that time. And after that we saw that what we were facing locally in Birmingham was really a national phenomenon that these were the children for whom— for whatever the reason—the systems just were not working, and their life chances were slim to none.

And we were absolutely convinced that these schools would offer these children something special—that children living in darkness would see a great light, and they would have hope. And so we came and started this program so that we could serve parents like the one who wrote the letter that we received when we were providing tuition assistance. It was a mother, a single mom who became a mother at 14, grew up in the public housing. Her mother, like her, had become a mother when she was a young teen. She said her mother never even finished grade school. And now this mother had three children living in public housing sending them to one of our most dismal-performing school districts in the nation.

Of the 78 schools in this particular urban school district, 64 were under academic probation. But this mother somehow managed to be able to get an apartment so she could move to another district and put her children in this school because she believed that education was the key to their success. It was the hope for her children.

But when she put them there, she said she discovered that her 14-year-old, who was going into the ninth grade, had to be placed in special education. And she said, "But he was doing so well. I don't understand. What happened?" And then describing the pain that she felt as she had to explain to this young fellow why he had to go into different classes and why he had to be labeled as such. But she said she was willing to do it for her children, whatever it took.

And then she wrote, "Can you imagine the pain I felt when I lost the apartment and had to move into the projects and put my children into the same school, the same system that had failed them?" And she was so grateful, she said, to learn of the scholarship that we were offering so that she could put her children in a Christian school, a school that would make a difference in the lives of her children.

> **"Why do you think I was leaving the house every day to go clean other people's houses? I was determined that my boys were going to get a good education." This mother sounds like so many other mothers that I've heard. Despite their circumstances, despite their conditions, they only want something better for their children and this firm belief that better is through a quality education.**

And her letter reminded me so much of my own story. I also was born in public housing in the projects in Mobile, Alabama. And while I was working on my doctorate, I was doing a history of faith-based schools that served minority children in the inner cities and in the rural areas when the public schools either were not available to them or would not work for them.

And so I called my mother in Mobile, Alabama at that time. And I said, "Mama, didn't we start out in a private school?"

And my mother—you could hear it in her voice saying "Oh, yes." She said, "All of you did." I had four brothers. She said, "Faith Lutheran Academy." She still had the little school pictures that we took. She said, "As a matter of fact, your oldest brother graduated from the Lutheran school."

I said, "Well, why did you do that?"

She said, "Well, you've got to understand the one public school that you could attend in Mobile, Alabama, at the time in the '50s, because of the laws of segregation, the one public school that you could attend was in such terrible condition I was determined that you would not go to that school because," she said, "I believed that an education was the way out of the projects. And I was determined that my boys were going to get a good education." This is from a mother who herself had only been afforded an eighth-grade education.

"But," I said, "We were living in the projects. Didn't it cost you? How could you afford that?"

And the next statement my mother made as I hung up the phone fighting back the tears moved me so deeply that right there I prayed. I said, "Father, if it pleases you, allow me to spend the rest of my life doing this."

Because my mother said, "Oh, yes, it cost me. Why do you think I was leaving the house every day to go clean other people's houses? I was determined that my boys were going to get a good education." She further said, "None of my boys were going to grow up to be ditch diggers." This mother sounds like so many other mothers that I've heard. Despite their circumstances, despite their conditions, they only want something better for their children and this firm belief that that better is through a quality education.

And to see these schools being closed at the level, at the rates at which they're closing, to see these centers of hope disappearing reminds me of the Hebrew writer who said, "Hope deferred makes the heart sick." And I ask the question, if the deferred hope sickens the heart, what happens to a heart where there's no hope? Thank you.

VIRGINIA WALDEN-FORD

Hello. I am so happy to be here. In the '50s I grew up in Little Rock, Arkansas. I'm one of five girls. As Vernard said he was one of five boys, I'm one of five girls of public school teachers, so my whole life has been about education.

Like Phylicia, I tried to get as far away from it as I could because I know how hard my parents struggled to raise us and to instill in us how important education was. And I wanted money, you know, so I was going to get a big job working somewhere and show off to the rest of the world. But I kept being pulled back into education. I'd look around and I'd see my friend's children struggling through school. And then when I had my own family I saw my own children struggling.

I was very blessed because my two older children were really gifted or driven and were able to navigate through the public school system that was really troubling in Washington, D.C. And they found mentors and programs and all kinds of things.

But with my third child, he was a victim. He became a victim of everything bad that you hear about in D.C., all the stereotypes. He was not particularly academically driven. He's smart but he'd rather play ball and ride his bike than go to school. He was one of those kinds of kids that was argumentative and got in trouble sometimes in school, actually got in trouble a lot in school. And people would say, "He's a bad kid."

I was given a gift of a scholarship for William to attend any school in Washington, D.C. that I chose. And I chose Archbishop Carroll High School because I really wanted him in an environment of faith. I wanted him somewhere where he would be protected. And it changed our lives.

And I would say, "No, he's not a bad kid. He needs to be challenged more." The joke in our family is that—my mother did say this to me, she said, "Honey, you'd better stay alive, because nobody will take William and raise him."

And I thought what a terrible thing, but it was a joke … but kind of true. But when he was 13, we were living in D.C. I was raising three kids as a single parent. And I was given a gift of a scholarship for William to attend any school in D.C. that I chose. And I chose Archbishop Carroll High School because I really wanted him in an environment of faith. I wanted him somewhere where he would be protected, and it changed our lives.

Every time he walks in the door and I see him, I realize how fortunate I was, because raising children in the mean streets of D.C. is tough, and there are so many obstacles for children of color, especially males. And so when he walks in the door now and kisses me on the cheek, I'm grateful that he's still here.

Well, this delight in my family gave me an opportunity to look at my life and say, "What can I do to help?" Other people need to be able to experience this kind of joy, to see their child just do well. And I was blessed to be able to found D.C. Parents for School Choice, which is a clearinghouse organization for primarily low-income families to get education information. And it was fun. It was great working with the parents.

And then in 2003, when we thought we could get a scholarship program passed in D.C.—at least I thought we could get a scholarship program passed in D.C.—we began to organize parents. And we started listening to their stories about how their children were dying in the streets and how they never knew how many kids would come home in the evening because the radio said, "black male was killed somewhere or a black girl was killed somewhere," and I still call my kids to make sure they're okay, even though they're adults now, because it's terrifying. You know, it's scary, and the schools were not protecting them. We were hearing as much about violence inside the schools as we were anywhere else.

Well, once the scholarship program was implemented—passed and was implemented—I also had the privilege of working with parents to find schools. What we found is that many of them were choosing faith-based schools. We were encouraging them to go to the other schools, and they really, really were choosing on a large scale Catholic schools in their communities. And the reason they were choosing those schools was because they believed two things. One, they would get a quality education, and two, God was in the house and would protect them, and they believed that very strongly.

And I remember we thought about it, and we talked about it, but it never became as clear to me as when we were converting some schools in Washington from Catholic schools to charter schools. And some groups of parents asked us to talk with them about it and what that meant and what charter schools would do.

We went armed with information about charter schools and how the conversion would be okay and that they would get the same kind of quality education … thinking that that's what they wanted. But what they really wanted was somebody to help them understand what they were going to do if their children were not in faith-based schools, if their children were not protected by having a spiritual base.

You know, one mother told me that she had lost one son to the streets of D.C. and now her surviving son, she wanted to keep him where he'd be safe, where he'd be taught about character and all those things that he needed to survive, she thought, in the streets. She was convinced that the public schools could not do that for him … or a charter school could not do that for him, and that was disturbing.

As parent organizers, we support trying to maintain these schools, trying to make sure that they survive, because, from what I hear from the parents, if we don't have this option for parents and children, it is going to change the direction of their lives.

And then we began to listen to other parents, and they were telling similar stories about how they really wanted their children in faith-based schools. Another mother who had been educated in a Christian school said she had five kids, and they were all in a Christian school in D.C. and that she picked that school because it was faith-based, even though she had to take two buses and the subway with her five babies to get there.

So I mean in D.C., in a place where so much violence and so many tragedies happen to children, this is a place where they can find peace. I remember William coming out of school the first two or three weeks, and I said to him, "Why are you being so good? You haven't been in trouble. Nobody's called to have me come get you."

And he said, "The people at the school care whether I learn or not. They care about me. They call me William, not 'hey you.' I feel safe." You know that was important to him, and he was a 13-year-old boy who seldom spoke that much, so you know this is what families are getting.

Last night I actually left the reception to go to a parent meeting, and the meeting was held at a Catholic school here in D.C. And when I walked in, parents were really excited and anxious to get started and talk to me about our legislative effort that's coming up to fight for reauthorization of our scholarship program. And I was tired. And as much as I love them, I was kind of ready to go home. Let me speak and go home.

And they got caught up, and they were testifying, and the spirit was in the room. And I got caught up because the place was jumping. This is what we need. You know, we need for our children to be in environments, especially in cities like D.C., where most of these kids leave school and go home and don't go out to play because there's too much violence outdoors.

So we as parent organizers or parent organizations, we support everybody in trying to maintain these schools and trying to encourage people to get out and make sure that they survive, because I'll tell you from what I hear from people out in the field and what I hear from the parents, if we don't have this option for parents and children, it is going to change the direction of their lives. If they have to go back into public schools, it will impact who they become.

So as we move forward, we want to do everything we can to assist faith-based organizations that are running schools, the Catholic Church (that) is running schools, and make sure that we stand beside them and continue. We are so blessed that we have a President that cares about this issue. He's always been supportive of the D.C. program, but to hear him up here this morning talking about how important this issue was to him inspired me to go on. It made me feel that I cannot stop until we make sure that this issue is addressed.

And he—like Phylicia—excited me. Like Vernard, he excited me. We all here care about what happens to these families. We are warriors on this stage, and we will continue to go on and fight the good fight, and we will have our children in faith-based schools.

Conclusion

Hein

Thank you so much. Thank you for your words and your inspiration. Thank you even more so for the way you serve real people in real time in real communities. The President did call us to action. He called (for) multi-sector solutions, as I referenced earlier in my remarks. But as government officials and as philanthropists and as business leaders, we cannot effectively deploy solutions unless we understand what it looks like in those communities and on the street. And you've provided that for us today, and we appreciate your service so very much.

LUNCH PLENARY: EDUCATION OPTIONS AND AMERICA'S CITIES

Secretary Margaret Spellings We are going to use our time wisely and take this opportunity to share some insights with three people I know well, all friends. And not only do they talk the talk, as they say, but they also walk the walk, and I've seen them do it.

Today with us (is) Secretary Roy Bernardi from Housing and Urban Development. He is the former mayor of Syracuse, a former Catholic school student. Likewise my friend, the former mayor of Indianapolis, Steve Goldsmith, who is quite a social entrepreneur, to quote the President from this morning, and my very good friend, Nancy Grasmick, who is the Chief State School Officer in Maryland, not far from here. And she is an active and vigorous education reformer on all fronts.

We all know why we are here, and the President talked this morning about our quest, our shared goal and dream of finding a high-quality education for every single student, wherever that might be. What we are here to talk about today are some very excellent examples of how that is taking place really all around the country.

And I'm going to start by asking my friend, Roy Bernardi, who, as I said, is from the Department of Housing and Urban Development. Actually we have done some partnerships with them on some of these things. He worked closely with faith-based schools when he was mayor of Syracuse and did some interesting things, and he's going to tell his story. And then we'll go to Steve.

Acting Secretary Roy Bernardi Thank you, Secretary Spellings.

Ladies and gentlemen, it's a pleasure to be here.

Madame Secretary, thank you for the good work that you do, working with principals and superintendents and teachers throughout the country to provide a quality education for every child. I also want to thank President Bush for putting this together, elevating support for the inner-city children and faith-based schools in our nation. Also my thanks go to the members of the panel, my fellow mayor, Stephen Goldsmith from Indianapolis, and Superintendent Nancy Grasmick from Maryland.

I've seen this issue from many perspectives. I'm a product of parochial school, K through 12, in Syracuse, New York. I was a public school high school teacher for four years, a guidance counselor in a public high school for three years. I was also mayor of the City of Syracuse, as the Secretary indicated. And now I'm the Acting Secretary for the Department of Housing and Urban Development.

I want to make one thing very, very clear. If anyone thinks that the health of our cities is not directly related to our parochial schools, they're very sadly mistaken. Now, the public schools do the heavy lifting, and I'm sure Nancy will give you those numbers in Maryland. Ninety percent of all K through 12 students are educated in the public school system, but the parochial schools obviously play a very critical role.

I want to make one thing very, very clear. If anyone thinks that the health of our cities is not directly related to our parochial schools, they're very sadly mistaken.

How do they play that critical role? First, by offering quality education, and that's just not in the early grades. In high school, parochial schools, 98 percent of the students graduate and 97 percent go on to higher education.

Second, the parochial schools offer opportunity. They reach millions of underprivileged children, especially in the inner cities, and the overwhelming majority of those children are not Catholic, but they're provided with a quality education, quality education at a lower cost. And I've always said I think the children, the kids in the cities, deserve the same opportunity as the children in suburbs.

And finally, these schools offer structure. And if you've attended parochial school, you'll know what I mean by that structure. The Franciscans are the ones that taught me. And what I didn't get at home I got there, not only in education, but in socialization and in discipline. But that tough love is a great antidote to life out on the streets. As a former mayor, I can tell you with gangs and children with nothing to do, idle time—that can be quite a problem.

Now, at HUD we try to make sure that public housing doesn't fall into disrepair. It has to be the same way with our parochial schools. These schools today, as this conference is pointing out, need our help. Catholic school enrollment is down from 5 million in 1960 to about 2.3 million now. In 1998, the diocese in the city of Syracuse ran 49 schools. Today that's down to 29, and that's affected approximately 5,700 youngsters.

So how do we get it back? How do we give back? First, you work together as partners. Any mayor will tell you that it's Federal. It's State. It's local. It's not-for-profits. It's any group or organization that resides within your jurisdiction. I was always fond of telling anyone who would listen that if government had to do it alone, it would never get it done. It's the not-for-profit and the faith-based organizations that really, really make this country what it is.

When I was a mayor, I worked with a Father Joseph Champlin, who is now deceased. He created an endowment fund called the Guardian Angel Society for Cathedral School. They were K through 6 right in the heart of the city of Syracuse, predominantly African-American. We engaged the entire community. He came to me and asked for help. He said, "We are going to need the resources." And obviously, the government cannot give resources directly, but I'll talk to you a bit later about what you can do with a faith-based organization.

What we did is we contacted entrepreneurs. We contacted business people. We were able to create this foundation for resources. These children at Christmastime went to Radio City Music Hall to a show. We provided them with the opportunity for books, computers. And the school was very, very successful. How do I know that? Because there are two of those graduates at Georgetown right now, and these are kids that would not have had the opportunity if it had not been for Cathedral Academy.

In the fall of each year as mayor, we would hold a barbecue for the city of Syracuse, north, south, east, and west. And we would have contributors. We would have companies that would provide the hot dogs or a hamburger or a soda. There was also a company that would provide a backpack for every child. So these were not just the private schools, the parochial schools, but public schools as well. So the children going back would have the necessary tools they needed to get started.

So a strong community is a community that has variety. It has choice. Just as the housing crisis we now have in our country—you look at neighborhoods and you see a foreclosure. We don't want an empty school either, because a street and a neighborhood are all-encompassing, and the parochial school is an anchor of that neighborhood, always has been.

And I can recall my days as a student, but for the sake of time I won't get into that right now, but I just want to say that we look for innovative ideas. Some people would tell you there are no new ideas. Perhaps there aren't, but there's involvement. And the President's involved. The Secretary's involved. You're all involved, so we can look for ways in which we can make sure that the resources are there so that these children, especially inner-city youngsters, have the same opportunity. They have the same work. They have the same desires, the same goals and will achieve the same success. If we can provide resources to keep these schools open, there will be even more of them. Thank you.

Secretary Spellings Thank you, Roy.

Next up is Steve Goldsmith who, in addition to being the former mayor of Indianapolis, is the chairman of the Corporation for National and Community Service.

I have known Steve for a while, and I would just say that in Texas, we would say Steve was country before country was cool. That means he has been talking about these things and not only talking about them, but doing them for literally decades.

And, Steve, why don't you tell us about some of that history.

Honorable Steve Goldsmith Madame Secretary, I appreciate the attention that you and the President have focused on this important issue. And I really liked the remarks.

I saw someone from one of the foundations as I walked in. And it reminds me of kind of one of the more embarrassing moments of my life where I had this chance for this personal conversation with Milton Friedman, and I was talking about public schools. And he said, "No, you're talking about government schools. Public schools educate the public. Government schools are schools run by the government, right?"

That was an important moment in my education because, from that point on, I viewed my role as mayor as contributing to the public education opportunities of my citizens and the children in my city. And from that perspective then in our city, the range of religious schools and predominantly the Catholic schools in the inner-city were the stabilizing force for our neighborhoods. They provided an alternative, as the Secretary said, where parents could send their children, because as any mayor knows from one of the cities that is stressed, the path to the middle class is a path to the suburbs.

> **I took the State of the City address to a Roman Catholic school. I was trying to say that these are hard-pressed neighborhoods, and these inner-city religious schools are always in financial difficulty. And, in fact, the more they fulfill their social and moral initiative, the more money they lose. So it's a community responsibility that should be led by the secular leaders of a city, not just the religious leaders.**

People who grow up in the cities and have children view their options for schooling to move from the city. So the Catholic schools and the other religious schools were holding our communities together. In that regard, I haven't done an empirical evaluation, but my guess is I'm the only Jewish mayor to chair an archdiocese fundraising drive. It's a fair bet without any research.

And I took the state of the city address to a Roman Catholic school. And what I was trying to do is say these are hard-pressed neighborhoods, and these inner-city religious schools are always in financial difficulty. And, in fact, the more they fulfill their social and moral initiative, the more money they lose, right? So it's a community responsibility that should be led by the secular leaders of a city, not just the religious leaders.

We'll get into the questions and answers about what's the appropriate role for government and how to make a difference, but just an introductory remark. I think that one of the most important things we have to do, in part, started by the President's comments this morning, is to make the case that these are community issues to save these schools because saving these schools will save the children, as the Secretary mentioned. Thank you very much.

Secretary Spellings Thank you, Steve.

Our final panelist is Maryland's superintendant Nancy Grasmick, my friend and colleague. Nancy has had an amazing career in education, started as a special education teacher and is revered and maybe a little feared, which I love, in education circles in the entire community in Maryland. She is an awesome reformer. There is no tool that will go unused in Nancy's toolkit.

And I appreciate your great work. So, Nancy, tell us about the kinds of things you've done in Maryland to meet the needs of those communities.

Nancy Grasmick Well, thank you, Secretary Spellings, and this is a mutual admiration society. We are just simply lucky in this country to have Margaret Spellings. I know you agree with me. But today it's important to tell the unvarnished truth, and so in Maryland there is absolutely no appetite for vouchers or anything that even approximates a voucher. And so as I thought about that and the political situation, I decided there were ways in which we could work around this and attempt to help faith-based schools and nonpublic schools overall in terms of benefits to our children. And all of us gathered here today care about every child getting a high-quality public and private education.

And so in 1998 I decided to create a nonpublic work group where we invited not only the superintendents and representatives from our school systems, but also from our nonpublic schools. The group has been chaired by two people, one from the public school sector and one from the nonpublic school sector. And in a moment I'll tell you about the things they've tackled, but I have to say that the success of this has been very dependent on a few people, one the incredible leadership of the superintendent of the Catholic schools, Dr. Ronald Valenti, who's here with us today.

He is my friend and colleague. And often as I visit Catholic schools within the city, people say, "Why are you two so friendly?" Or we are on a radio show together. But we are constantly collaborating. And then we have a whole series of nonpublic special education schools that serve many of our city children. And so Dorie Flynn who's with us representing those nonpublic special education schools is another fabulous partner for us. So children are getting, in a timely way, the intense services they need.

In Maryland there is absolutely no appetite for vouchers. As I thought about that and the political situation, I decided there were ways we could work around this and attempt to help faith-based schools and nonpublic schools overall in terms of benefits to our children. All of us gathered here today care about every child getting a high quality public and private education.

And so as we looked at the issues, a huge issue was the idea that our nonpublic schools, particularly in the urban areas dealing with children who are economically disadvantaged, needed some textbook dollars that could also be used for technology. And with the leadership, particularly of Dr. Valenti and those from the Jewish community coming together, we were able to get almost $4 million a year to provide for those kinds of opportunities for our children in our nonpublic schools.

We also know that it is a chronic problem, and particularly in the urban areas because the public schools are very preoccupied with chronically underperforming schools, to ensure that dollars that are directed from the U.S. Department of Education are getting to our faith-based schools in a timely and appropriate manner. And so that is another area that we are tackling through this nonpublic work group. And just recently Dr. Valenti invited me to make a presentation to the mid-Atlantic group for the Catholic schools in terms of setting up a model that could be replicated literally throughout the country in terms of how we can ensure that every dollar that's deserved goes to the faith-based schools.

We also have a very exciting record in Maryland for our supplemental educational services, and I think the national percentage is about 19 percent participation. We have 69 to 70 percent participation, and we are very careful in terms of the applications and ensuring that our faith-based providers have an opportunity to provide those services for our public school students. And so that's another exciting development.

And the other thing that has been very important, particularly in our Jewish community, given some of the cultural and religious aspects that have to be considered, is to provide parental choice services within those schools, and so we are doing that.

In addition, and finally I'll conclude with this, we are extremely interested in early identification and our infants and toddlers program, and so we are working with all of the nonpublic sectors to ensure those children are identified early and getting the intervention and services required. So it's been a very exciting time to work this nonpublic work group in a State where there is a political inhibition to having any kind of direct contribution of dollars other than these nonpublic textbook and technology dollars. Thank you.

Questions and Discussion

Secretary Spellings That is such a really great point and, I think, a jumping off point to some of our discussions. I want to mention one thing about supplemental services that you all might not be aware of. Just this week, a couple days ago, in Detroit in fact, I announced some new regulations from the Department of Education which will be coming into final effect before year-end. And as those of you who have thought about providing supplemental services in your communities, you know that there are some significant disincentives in the public schools to use those dollars in those ways.

So we are going to make that more attractive to the public school community by saying, "You can roll it over for one year, but if you don't spend the money on those kids," because not everybody has a 70 percent take-up rate, "then those moneys come back to the U.S. Treasury."

So I think that will cause some great things to occur out there, and your phones might be ringing a little more vigorously in light of that.

All right, Steve, let us start with you. Since you've been doing this a long time, I know there are some things you've learned along the way. How do you bring communities together around lofty goals in places that might have some of the resistance that Nancy has talked about?

Mayor Goldsmith Well, I think unfortunately, most places have some resistance to the right. Let me just talk for a second about specific tools. So it seems the beginning point is a high-level key recognition that the mission of the religious school is critical to the future of the city. That everybody is in this. It's not just Catholic, Jewish, or particular Christian or Evangelical schools important to the cities.

> **Religious schools actually subsidize public schools, because you're educating a child who otherwise would have to be educated with the full cost to the public. So this is not a transfer of resources from taxpayers to religious schools. It's a way to help the religious schools continue their subsidies.**

Second then, if you view your role as educating children, then as Nancy suggested, there's a range of tools that are available. We were proud to have started an effort where we used the city's tax-exempt debt issuance authority to finance the remodeling and opening of new schools. There are financial advisors I know that provide advice to the Catholic schools without complicated financial ledgers that can actually turn the schools, which are embedded assets, into a way to support the children, and the city can play a role.

If you've reached that point where you ought to say—and many larger cities are like this—transportation should be funded for children, and transportation should not be just to a public school. Special classes could be offered in the public schools for children who are in the religious schools, because these are services, public education services for those children—or textbooks. And you can fill in that.

Let me just diverge. You all know this, but I doubt that many of our citizens know it, that religious schools actually subsidize the public schools, because you're educating a child who otherwise would have to be educated with the full cost of the public. So this is not a transfer of resources from taxpayers to religious schools. It's a way to help the religious schools continue their subsidies.

And a last comment, I mean there are some other structures, and Nancy is heroic in her work, but if you don't have her in all 50 States, hypothetically, there are other structures. The Pennsylvania corporate tax credit program is a very good one (for more, see "Tax Credits" in the main report). It allows corporations to make contributions that are tax-deductible that will help fund the children. So there are a lot of things that can be done.

I also was proud to be on the board of our private voucher program, the Charitable Choice Program. I was totally supportive of our public schools. The point is not to erode the public schools. It is to provide competitive alternative choices for parents who wanted those. And so whether we raised the voucher money, whether we diverted the transportation dollars, if you will, or whether we did financing for the religious schools, all of those made for more vibrant communities which helped educate our children better.

Secretary Spellings Nancy, you talked a little about the working group. What are the kinds of conditions that had to be in place to make sure that could be successful? I saw a lot of heads nodding, saying, "That sounds like something we could do." What do you need to make sure happens so that that thing can work?

Grasmick Well, I really think you have to forge a relationship. It won't work if there are these stovepipe attitudes and polarization. And so I think it was born of the relationship that Dr. Valenti and I have and have had for so many years and the idea that our nonpublic special education schools—we certainly invite into it our independent schools, but there had to be a working relationship.

And I have to say this. It's not a compliment to me, but people are simply amazed that in Maryland every year all of the nonpublic entities have a huge breakfast for me because of the collaboration, and we bring up issues that we are committed to resolving together. And there is a huge level of respect, and so I think that has to be a fundamental issue.

It's not just at the work group but that it follows through in terms of the daily work of the individuals. I think there have to be certain targets. And certainly we look at all of the State laws, all of the local laws and the interpretation of those and how those laws can benefit our nonpublic schools, not again, as you suggested, to erode in any way the public schools, but how those laws can be interpreted fairly to not deprive the nonpublic schools of opportunities. And I think the idea of our coming together around the idea of the nonpublic textbook and technology moneys and my sitting there every year in the general assembly when they're deliberating as to whether or not these dollars should continue.

And we are very skillful in not giving the message that we are not supportive to public schools but also that we administer those funds. We are excited about the testimony and what's happening relative to those funds, so we administer every dollar of those funds in our department. We identify specific people who work with the schools. We develop the application for it so that there's this constant engagement, which I think is so exciting.

Secretary Spellings You were talking about kind of a broad agenda from technology and textbooks to early childhood. How did your group come together on particular priorities at a given time?

Grasmick Well, a lot of it has to do with issues that they're grappling with at any particular time. One of the big issues is our nonpublic special education schools and the idea of our whole continuum from infants and toddlers through high school and how do we identify these children who may be in faith-based schools or in child care settings? So that they will bring the topics to the chairs, to the group, and there's agreement in terms of what we are pursuing. And I think it is born of the idea: What are the most current issues that have to be dealt with?

Dr. Valenti brought to my attention the idea that the title dollars were not necessarily going to nonpublic schools in an effective and fair manner. We have to grapple with that. We've worked together to set up a model and to pursue that model across the State.

Secretary Spellings I'd like to know more about that. Thank you, Nancy. Well said.

Roy, obviously the mayor is often the focal point of helping educate the public, the big bully pulpit. You talked about some of the closings of schools you had in Syracuse. How can a mayor engage and have a community better understand what's at stake with our faith-based schools, and what are things that mayors can do to guard against those closures?

Acting Secretary Bernardi Well, first and foremost is to understand the problem before it happens. Probably most of you read last Sunday's Washington Post. In Petersburg, Virginia, St. Joseph's Catholic School was going to close, and the dioceses there gave them, I think, a week to raise a million dollars. Well, the good news is that as of this Monday they raised a million dollars to remain open.

I would ask everyone in this room to make sure that you access not just the Department of Housing and Urban Development, but also the faith-based offices that the President has put throughout the federal government so you can access those funds. There are resources there, so I would ask you to take advantage of them.

And how that happens is how a mayor will tackle the problem regardless of where you are in this country, is that you have to engage everyone. Information is power. The fact of the matter is there are parochial schools that have closed in this country, and they didn't know that until the last possible moment. And I think everyone needs an opportunity to bring the shakers and movers in the community together to see if you can save those schools.

You talked about how you access dollars, and that's the name of the game regardless of where you are. Well, the Department of Housing and Urban Development in 2004, our faith-based office, we held around the country grant-writing training programs. Over 30,000 individuals participated. In 2008, we plan this year to have 50 locations for those grant-writing programs. And I bring this up to make sure that your local communities access that grant-writing training program, because it's how you put that application together.

And we don't preclude religious organizations. Obviously, they should not be precluded. The fact of the matter remains on the receiving of the grant, as long as it's not used for a specific religious purpose, you can apply. So I would ask everyone in this room to make sure that you access not just the Department of Housing and Urban Development, but also faith-based offices that the President has put throughout the federal government so that you can access those funds, the community development block grant moneys and the home moneys. There are resources that are there, so I would ask you to take advantage of them.

Secretary Spellings All right. It's time for your questions. While you are coming to the microphone, let me ask Steve real quickly as mayor. Obviously, engaging the community and making the case that we ought to care about all schools is something that I think you did it. Steve, do you want to talk a little about that while our questioners are coming forward?

Mayor Goldsmith Well, I think putting together a high-level effort with representatives throughout the community is helpful. I mean we had a terrific archbishop. We had some very strong Christian school leaders. And we had, I think probably most importantly, neighborhood leaders who were outspoken that this school is stabilizing our neighborhood. And so it's the combination. And I was mayor long enough that we had a lot of school superintendents come and go, but most of them were supportive of the effort, because they knew that they wanted to hold children and have families live in the city.

Putting together a high-level effort with representatives throughout the community is helpful. We had a terrific archbishop. We had some very strong Christian school

leaders. We had, probably most importantly, neighborhood leaders who were outspoken that this school is stabilizing our neighborhood.

So if I think you have high-level leadership, grass-roots support, and you make the case—the financial information as well as the performance information needs to be out there—that is the groundwork around which dollars can be moved and raised and new laws passed.

Audience Member Madame Secretary, Joe McTighe from CAPE, the Council for American Private Education. First of all, it's a wonderful forum, and it's been focusing the spotlight on an absolutely critical issue, and we are very grateful for that, and we appreciate that. But one of the recurring themes today has been that at a time when the country desperately needs successful inner-city schools, it makes no sense whatsoever to stand by and watch schools that have a track record of success close down in record numbers.

But if we are going to address that issue at the policy levels—and I'm talking specifically at the Federal level now—it's going to take a serious bipartisan effort, I think, similar to what took place when No Child Left Behind was initially enacted and also similar to what's going on right now in terms of addressing the housing crisis. Is there a way that the Administration can facilitate a dialog at the highest levels in Congress, bipartisan dialog to address this particular crisis?

One of the recurring themes today has been that at a time when the country desperately needs successful inner-city schools, it makes no sense whatsoever to stand by and watch schools that have a track record of success close down in record numbers.

Secretary Spellings Well, I'll start. I would say that in a Presidential election year, that's a hard time to do it, just candidly. But I would also say that I do think, when we look at the compelling data, our shared commitment to leave no child behind and the way that the President has proposed and formulated this $300 million effort (Pell Grants for Kids) that makes us ask are we for real about No Child Left Behind or not? Because we've given schools every possible opportunity to improve. Now what?

And so I think the moral imperative is there. I think politically, frankly, this has to be motivated—all politics is local, as we all know—back home around the needs of particular regions and communities. Only then will the Nancy Grasmicks of the world have the kind of climate to think outside those usual structures.

I will tell you that I think data and accountability are our greatest friends in this effort. That's why there's such fierce opposition to put that elephant back in the closet, to stop peeling the onion, to make everybody feel that all is well. So stay strong for data and motivate politics back home I think is what I would do.

Mayor Goldsmith You know the answer to this. I'm just a local guy. So I would say, though, that your earlier comment about the SES program focuses on the fact that the President's faith-based initiative ended a significant amount of regulatory discrimination against faith-based organizations. And that is what this conference is supposed to do—but that concept, applied to existing revenue streams, would lead to substantial results.

And I agree with you, Madame Secretary, that's probably the best you would accomplish in an election year.

But that's not—as the HUD program suggests—an insignificant amount of money, and it would make a little bit of a difference in at least bridging and reducing some of the closures until we get to a bolder point.

Secretary Spellings The other thing is, I think, as we talked about Pennsylvania and other places with tax credit policies. You know, sometimes those are less incendiary politically than some of the other things that we've talked about, so don't neglect your State legislature. Funding for education is nine cents from the federal government and 91 cents from State and local government. And it's the old "He who has the gold makes the rules" philosophy. And so State legislatures obviously—the President talked a little bit about Blaine amendments—certainly should not be overlooked.

Audience Member Jim Cultura from the New York State Catholic Conference. I think many of us are surprised but intrigued that as former mayors, you've made the point that the strength of our schools has an effect on the economic and social strength of cities. And obviously there are a small number of mayors, current mayors in the country, who have come out in support of school choice.

Do you think it's politically possible to get the mayors nationwide as a group, like the conference of mayors in New York which we've tried to approach, to get them to come out in support of school choice, to get away from this notion that it's us versus them, private schools versus public schools, and talk about it in a broader sense as you've done on the social and economic strength of cities?

Acting Secretary Bernardi You're absolutely correct. As a former president of the New York State Conference of Mayors … Not just New York State, but any State, if they would take folks like yourself and conferences like this … Someone earlier mentioned the mortgage crisis. Why are we dealing with the mortgage crisis? Because it is a crisis! Well, I think we have a crisis right here in front of us with the closure of parochial schools and the opportunity for youngsters in the inner-city to have that quality education.

Why are we dealing with the mortgage crisis? Because it is a *crisis*! Well, I think we have a crisis right here in front of us with the closure of parochial schools and the opportunity for youngsters in the inner-city to have that quality education.

So reach out and talk to the various groups and organizations, the National League of Cities, Conference of Mayors, your local representatives, the Federal representatives. It's not going to happen unless the emphasis is put on it, but I cannot stress importantly enough what I talked about, accessing the programs that we have now.

There are resources out there, and those resources should not be limited just to the folks that have had access to those over the years. Faith-based organizations are participating more and more, but you need to do even more of that. Apply for those resources. Use those resources to help the schools that we are talking about.

Mayor Goldsmith I would just add that a little of it depends on what you mean by the word "choice." So if I think the word "choice" means voucher, the answer to your question is no. We might find a mayor in Milwaukee 10 years ago who favored it or in D.C. with Tony Williams, but very unusual. I think, though, the frame needs to be remade. These schools in our city, which is not atypical, the Catholic schools were 85 percent inner-city non-Catholics. This was a social mission and moral mission on the part of the church, and they were educating students in our community.

This debate can easily be reshaped around the opportunities for children, community development, and helping schools educate all faiths. If you did it that way, you could get a lot of mayors to say yes. But if they hear the word "choice" and they translate to it vouchers, I think the answer is no.

And I think the problem becomes that suburban parents have choices, and they don't see the faces of the kids in the urban areas. And the urban parents don't have much power, and they're unable to break through entrenched interests.

So it seems to me that if the framework changes, and it is community stabilization, and it is holding a city together … let me interrupt my thought. Secretary Spellings knows better than anybody else the horrible dropout rates of inner-city schools on the public school side. So I think this debate can easily be reshaped to be around a mission of future opportunities for children, community development, helping schools educate all faiths. And I think if you did it that way, and wanted to advocate Catholic or Jewish or Christian schools as an alternative, you could get a lot of mayors to say yes. But if they hear the word "choice" and they translate to it vouchers, I think the answer is no.

Audience Member Mary Ellen Russell from the Maryland Catholic Conference. One thought I've been having all morning that I don't think we've talked a lot about is the issue of benefits for teachers. We saw an extraordinary chart this morning (see Figure 10 in the main report) that's no secret to the Catholic schools about the shift from what we are calling practically free labor to trying to pay salaries for our teachers, and I think it's a critically important component of the crisis that we are facing now.

And I wondered in your wisdom, at the Federal level, at the State level, at the city level, any thoughts about how to supplement what our schools can do to help our teachers to include them in programs or ways that would help us to compensate those teachers?

Grasmick Mary Ellen and I worked together on some of these initiatives, but I do think health care is so costly today, and joining a larger cohort, getting a reduced rate, things like that where we could come together to look at collective benefits, I think, could be enormously helpful. So Mary Ellen, I make a commitment. I'd be glad to work with you in attempting to look at some of these things, because I think doing it individually is just economically killing these schools.

Secretary Spellings I would just offer one thought at the moment. Again, of course, the things that we are talking about, pay for performance and vouchers, these are the holy grails of education, so we've given ourselves a lot to bite off, as you all know. One of the things that the President has supported and the unions have tried desperately to kill actually is a hundred million dollar program called the Teacher Incentive Fund. He's asked to double this program.

And the notion is: Let us find ways to pay people who do the most challenging work in education and get results. Currently there are about 40 of these models going on around the country that align that hardest work with pay incentives. And we are just beginning to develop this practice. That obviously can be shared and replicated as it's developed, but also we can potentially look, as we work to expand those things, that some of those dollars be made available to the challenging work that's going on in our nonpublic schools.

Mayor Goldsmith I have no idea what the answer to your question is, but I used to be a politician, so I'm going to answer it anyway. Another way to look at it, in addition to the appropriate comments that were just made, is to say: How can you reduce noncritical teacher costs in order to drive more money to the teachers. And that means better financing of the buildings. It means highly specialized classes that only have only a few students, those students ought to be able to enroll in the public school or charter school to secure those services.

So to the extent we can create a menu and disaggregate those services and move to the public side those that are legitimately public, it would allow more money to be driven into the teacher salaries as being core. It's not directly responding to your question, but perhaps another way to think about it, like transportation.

Audience Member Good afternoon. I'm Dorie Flynn. I'm from Maryland, so mine is more of a comment than a question. But I just wanted to mention that the leadership that we have in Dr. Grasmick has really made the partnership between public and nonpublic work so well.

Something that Dr. Grasmick mentioned in her opening remarks was the commitment that she has to provide services to privately placed students. And so she helps coordinate and actually gives grant dollars to provide wraparound support and related services to the Jewish day schools. And we have a large concentration of Jewish day schools in Baltimore County, and I helped coordinate this project that gives speech and language services to kids, to Jewish day school kids, to keep them in their faith-based schools. So it's more just about a compliment to you, and we appreciate your support.

Secretary Spellings Thank you all for your participation and your good work.

In: Disadvantaged Students and Crisis in…
Editor: Thomas G. Wilson

ISBN: 978-1-60741-535-0

Chapter 5

Panel III: Community Solutions

The White House Domestic Policy Council

Scott Hamilton

Welcome. We are going to continue this terrific program today with a fantastic panel, a number of whom you have already heard about at least from the President if not in other ways. And there's full text or a portion of the materials for the conference, and I commend them to you.

My name is Scott Hamilton, and I am thrilled to be a part of this conference. In my experience, faith is necessary and truly key to all who work successfully with our neediest students in all kinds of schools, public, private or religious. Surrounded by the challenge, the struggle, the occasional failure, it is hard for many educators not to eventually surrender to low expectations. It's hard for us all. And it is certainly hard, as we've seen, for some not to begin to blame all the other factors.

We've seen the defenders of the status quo, and many who are defenders of the failing government school systems claim that we can only succeed in schools if we solve poverty or solve health care or solve all number of ailments. But the bottom line I believe we all share is that education is a place to start.

I was lucky enough to have worked with KIPP for about five years and started the effort to replicate two terrific schools, which has now turned into more than 50 schools, and I learned a lot from that experience. And very recently I was lucky to have had the opportunity to lead a study for the Thomas B. Ford Institute on the revival of urban Catholic schools.

And what I've learned from those two experiences are two things. There is a great philosopher who once said that the actual proves the possible, and he was right. And it is necessary, especially in the face of those challenges, that we prove the possible through the actual. And the other thing that I have learned is that catchy little phrase that nothing succeeds like success. We cannot sit here committed to our goals and just wish that we could change policy or wish that these streams of funding that we so desperately need or want would appear. We have to get out of ourselves. We have to create the success that will attract that kind of support.

So on this panel today we have inspiration in the midst of our struggle, and we have reminders of what can be accomplished with vision and leadership, hard work, and yes, faith. They are examples of what growth and initiative can bring even in the tough business that we all share. So our panel of five is actually proving the possible, and they're going to share with you what can be done, have some ideas about how we can help our case and help ourselves and share some experiences learned.

And I encourage them at the conclusion of their remarks to ask each other questions as they arise, and I encourage you to keep in mind what questions come up that you'd like to ask if we have time at the end of the presentations for questions.

To begin, we have Mary McDonald, whom you heard about a little earlier in the President's remarks, has done remarkable things for the Jubilee Schools in Memphis.

Next is Tom Tillapaugh. He's got a remarkable story to tell with the street schools that he started and is replicating now.

B.J. Cassin is really the driving force behind the growth and reputation of the Cristo Rey and NativityMiguel networks of schools.

Reverend Timothy Scully is behind what you also heard the President talk about, the ACE program at Notre Dame and some other extraordinary initiatives that that university is undertaking.

And Rabbi David Zwiebel is doing remarkable things with the Agudath Israel organization and has some terrific remarks on philanthropy that we can all learn from.

So please help me welcome this panel and Dr. Mary McDonald.

MARY MCDONALD

Thank you for the opportunity to introduce you to the Jubilee Catholic Schools in the Diocese of Memphis. The Jubilee Schools are reopened Catholic schools in the inner-city. They are schools that have been closed from eight to more than 50 years.

When we left these schools, we left more than old buildings behind. We left children, children in poverty, children of a new immigrant population, children who needed a Catholic education now more than ever. We needed to go back and reclaim our heritage in educating those who were disenfranchised by society. Even though most thought it was impossible, we found courage in knowing that with God, all things are possible.

> **The Jubilee Schools are reopened Catholic schools in the inner city. They are schools that had been closed from eight to more than 50 years. When we left these schools, we left more than old buildings behind. We left children, children in poverty, children of a new immigrant population. When I started as superintendent, we had 15 schools, and five of those were struggling to survive. Now we have 29 schools and our highest enrollment since 1976.**

When Bishop Steib appointed me as superintendent of schools in 1998, he shared his desire to have the Catholic schools return to the neighborhoods and children we once abandoned and reclaim our heritage of lifting up children and families in poverty. So after months of planning, hard work, long hours, and the generosity of donors who gave us the seed money to begin, in July 1999, we started the reopening of the Jubilee Catholic Schools.

Like most dioceses across the country, the Diocese of Memphis was closing Catholic schools in the urban areas. This was due to the declining enrollment, lack of funding, and demographic shifts. Initially elementary schools were closed. Without Catholic feeder schools, several high schools were closed or consolidated.

When I started as superintendent, we had 15 schools, and five of those were struggling to survive. Now we have 29 schools and our highest enrollment since 1976. Our students in the Jubilee Schools come from the neighborhoods in which the schools are located. We do not test for entrance and welcome children regardless of religion or ability to pay tuition.

These schools are located in areas with some of the highest rates of poverty, illiteracy, crime, gang activity, and violent death in the country. The children are victims of their surroundings. Most are raised by a single female with little or no means of support, but poverty does not mean a parent does not love their child. Poverty means there are no choices for her child.

Each Jubilee School was reopened with a preschool and kindergarten class and added a grade a year to the exit level of sixth or eighth grade. You cannot solve a systemic problem with a programmatic approach. In order to effect systemic change, to change the universe for these children, we had to provide a new experience, a new paradigm for education.

We started in August of 1999 with one school and 26 children. Now we have eight Jubilee schools, two urban initiative schools, and more than 1,400 students (Figure 10). We are still adding grades in schools and still growing.

To ensure the systemic change that we sought, it is important that the students be educated in a Catholic school from preschool through 12th grade, so the financial assistance follows the students to each level of their education at the Catholic school. Every family pays something according to their ability to do so. It is their investment in their child's education.

More than 95 percent of our Jubilee school families are at or below the poverty level. This is serious poverty, particularly in comparison to the Shelby County median household income. Our schools are authentically Catholic, and the students attend daily religion class, Mass, and paraliturgical services. The faith traditions of all students are respected and celebrated.

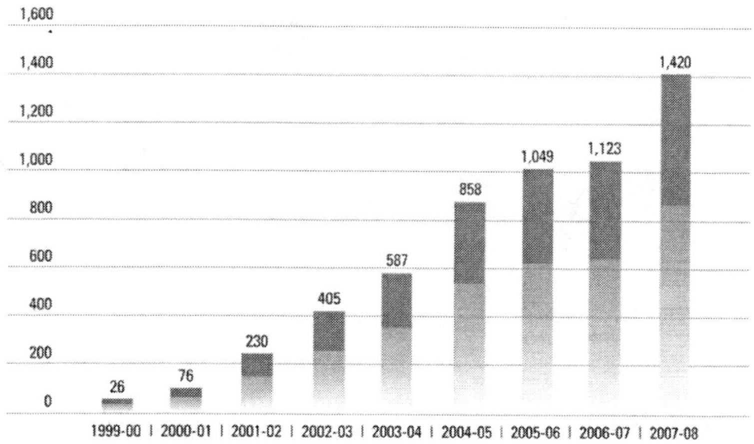

Mary McDonald, "White House Summit on Inner-City Children and Faith Based Schools," (presentation, The White House, Washington, D.C., April 24, 2008).

Figure 10. Jubilee Schools Enrollment

ITBS Reading

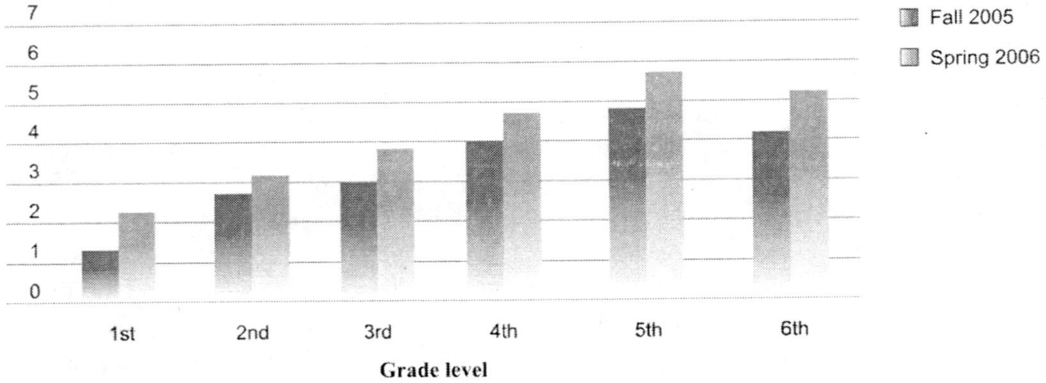

ITBS Language

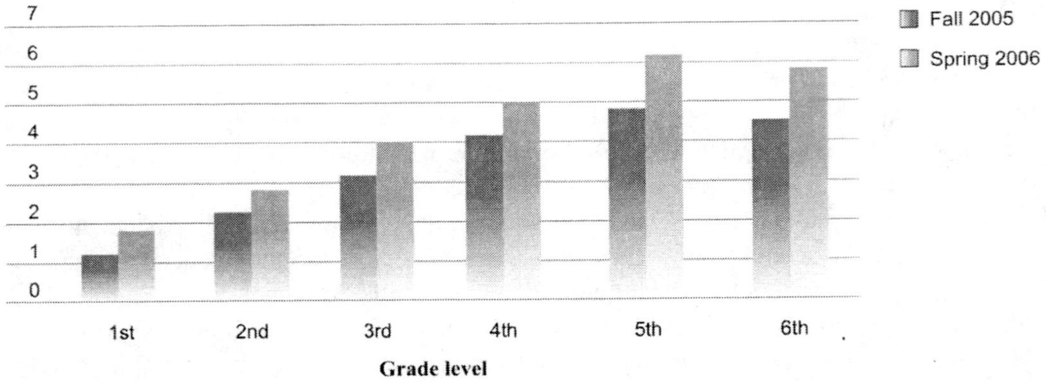

ITBS Math

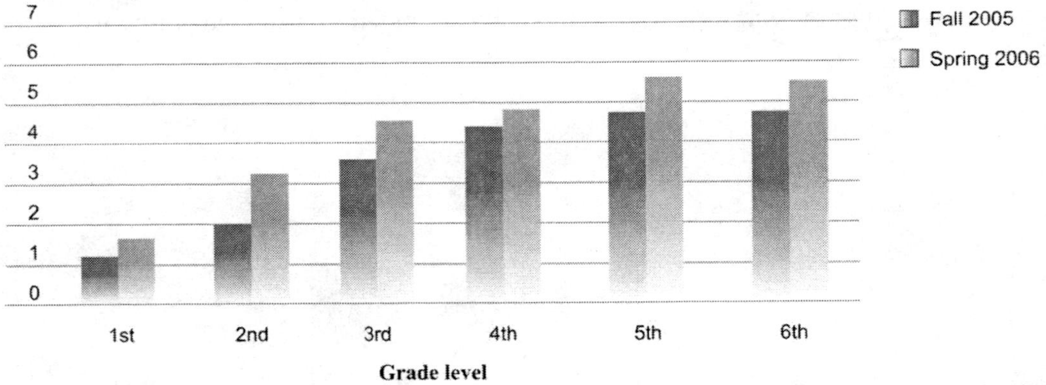

Mary McDonald, "White House Summit on Inner-City Children and Faith Based Schools," (presentation, The White House, Washington, D.C., April 24, 2008).
Sample scores from De La Salle Blessed Sacrament School.

Figure 11. Jubilee Schools Success Iowa Test of Basic Skills Grade Equivalent Scores

The Jubilee schools are considered community treasures and have done much to bridge the racial divide in Memphis. With only a 4 percent Catholic population, the schools also have shown the community how the church has reached out in service to all God's children.

Urban initiative schools are two inner-city Catholic schools that struggled against all odds to stay open, and now they receive Jubilee scholarship dollars each year to assist nearby low-income students to attend one of these schools. It is equally important that Catholic schools in urban areas are assisted in remaining open.

The intense daily hardships experienced by families living in poverty are barriers that diminish a parent's ability to fully provide the time, energy, and guidance necessary for strong education. The Jubilee schools are a resource for parents to use to overcome the obstacles that they face in their struggle to provide for their children.

The Jubilee schools are proof positive that poverty does not equate with ignorance. Most of our students come to us with few language skills and are functioning two or more years below grade level. However, within their first year in a Catholic school, significant academic advances are accomplished. Outside research confirmed the positive results of our students' success. The success of our students is borne out in many ways, a zero percent dropout rate, a 99.9 percent graduation rate, and 95 percent of our students continue their education in postsecondary schools. They are beating the odds. Their universe is changing. Their intergenerational cycle of poverty is being broken (Figure 11).

We learned early on that we first had to address the issues of hunger, of emotional distress, anger, fear, sleep deprivation—all the adverse effects of poverty that victimize the children—as well as teach them. Addressing the issues of hunger and unemployment was critical. For many, the food at school was their only meal of the day. In order to help the children, we partnered with the Food Bank and local businesses to provide students with backpacks every Friday filled with nutritious nonperishable food to eat and to share at home over the weekend.

We also started job training and placement programs for adults who are considered unemployable. We provide training, certification, and jobs in our cafeteria that lead to future employment in better-paying jobs.

Each parent or guardian and each student signs a pledge that holds them accountable for positive involvement in the educational process. The Catholic Schools Office is also held accountable to provide the professional management system and broad base of support needed to ensure the viability of these schools. During the past 10 years, the Catholic Schools Office has worked to move from a caretaker stage to accreditation by SACS/CASI as a fully functioning school district.

But we cannot do this alone. We need the involvement of many others. We have formed partnerships with businesses, foundations, universities, and health care facilities, all people in the community. Bishop J. Terry Steib, Bishop of the Diocese of Memphis is a staunch supporter of Catholic education. And so we continue in faith to reclaim our heritage, these schools, and the children. Thank you.

TOM TILLAPAUGH

In 1984, I loaded up my wife and kids in an old 1970 LT and followed what I believe—and I think in this room I can say I know—was a vision from God to move to Denver, Colorado, and open a Christian school for homeless, troubled, and at-risk kids.

I'd been working in Christian education in the suburbs, and we couldn't take the kids that I really wanted to take. They said a Christian education is not for them. A Christian and a faith-based education are for everybody in some form or another. I was 30 years old in the eyes of the world and in my grandmother's a fool. She offered me her house if I would quit this silly nonsense and come and teach in a nice safe town, but no, I knew my calling.

My motivation for starting Street Schools was seeing so many young people dropping out because of the bad choices they had made, the circumstances of their lives, and the way the regular schools operated for those kinds of kids. So I thought, "How can we make a school an inviting place to produce success for these kids?"

So my wife and I had nothing. We lived in Section 8 housing and did what we could to survive, including dumpster diving and whatever else it took as I began to cast this vision out to whoever would listen to me. I was just a kid, 30 years old. What did I know? We were going to solve all the problems of the world. We brought in [homeless kids], started bringing them home with me. We had seven homeless living with us at one time. The city knocked on my door and said, "You can only have two at a time."

We've got two homeless right now at my house in Colorado. How did that happen? It's been many years later, and they're still there.

This girl came in. She was 19 years old. She was homeless. She doesn't know her dad. Her mom conceived her, birthed her, and then dropped her off at her grandparents' house, and she's never seen her since. I'm going to turn her into a superstar, and she's going to go to college and you're going to hear from her someday. I'm so excited about that.

Finally, a local businessman answered the call. He rented me a house in the worst part of town in Denver.

Then on May 13, 1985, I grabbed three street people who were wandering around on the street, and I said, "Let us go back and let us have high school." And the first guy was never tardy because he lived in the crawl space under the house. It was so cool. He was right there every day.

I don't know anything except to love kids. How do you run a nonprofit? I didn't know anything about operations and HR and accounting and all those boring things. And how was I going to pay the bills, including feeding my family? Then I learned about this thing called endowment, and all I knew to do was to share that heart and vision with others and hope that they would get excited enough to help me financially, so I just started speaking with people.

But my motivation for starting Street Schools was seeing so many young people dropping out because of the bad choices they had made and the circumstances of their lives and way the regular schools operated for those kinds of kids. So I thought how can we make a school an inviting place to produce success for these kids?

Well, first, smaller is better. In those days bigger was better. You can have all the labs and all the fancy things, but they don't do any good for kids who aren't there. Smaller is better, 50 to 90 kids is all that a principal can really know of that kind of challenging kid. These kinds of kids need 10 to one in the classroom.

And then the faculty is far more than teachers. I wanted teachers that were willing to go the extra mile. That's why I love KIPP so much, because they do. They're advocates. We have an advocate program, and every day they meet with those kids formally in the classroom and then lunch and after school and weekends. And they're engaged in their lives constantly, and they help the kids to catch a powerful vision for a successful future and then give them the tools to attain it. And that's what it takes.

By 1985, I began to receive calls from people in other cities saying, "I heard about what you're doing in Denver. Could you help me to do that in my city?" So ultimately we founded the National Association of Street Schools. It's a vehicle or a means by which to replicate this model around the country.

We have about 45 schools now, and we are part of the Bill and Melinda Gates Foundation's Alternative High School Initiative. We are the only faith-based group in that right now, so keep praying for us as we try to be witness to the rest of those people.

Street Schools initially served troubled kids, kids who had already manifested trouble. But as we started growing and growing our model, we began to realize that the best practices that we were advocating for worked for other people, people like Tim Cox who started a school in Memphis for the younger kids. A lot of people call it preventative. Get them while they're younger so they don't get in trouble in the long run.

Urban faith-based educational institutions are doing a tremendous job in serving the academic, social, emotional and spiritual needs of the children and adolescents of our nation's inner cities. It is imperative that we continue to find the funding needed to keep them open and viable.

You can read in your conference proceedings document the synopsis of our design model: Individualized academic development, diagnostic tests, sensitivity to different learning styles, high expectations. We are very big on economic literacy. We developed an urban economic literacy curriculum with college students, also personal social skills development. Like I said, I talk about advocates, and it's all about getting face time with the kids. And the more loving, caring help and wisdom—and help them as they work to make changes in their life—the more role models they'll have.

Career development: I became a teacher because my dad was a teacher. I didn't want to be, but you know so many times you become what your father is because that's what you observe every day. What if you don't have a father to observe? What if your father's in jail? What if he's an alcoholic or a drug addict? What do you do in those cases? And also what if all your friends in your neighborhood are in the same position?

So we have to be *in loco parentis* all the time in our school and teach our kids what to do when they grow up. So we have had shadowing internships that our kids do.

Spiritual development: A Street School is a Christian school. We believe that Jesus Christ gives hope and purpose in what can seem like a hostile, purposeless world, so we have Bible and chapel. Our kids go on mission trips to learn to serve others just as they're being helped.

When I started the Street School in '84 I didn't have a template to follow. Remember, I was just a kid, and so it took years of trial and error to figure things out. Our goal is to have a template so they won't have to go through all those years and they can be turn-key. So we do lots of things. We've been asked to do training, whether it be at our national conference or on site, anything, how to do a 501(c)(3) or all the major operations and HR and fundraising, a lot of fundraising training and so on.

Strategies for continuous school improvement: We have a continuum of elements and essentials for having quality urban Christian schools that our schools are continually doing, steps to a continuing improvement plan as they work through accreditation. We offer teachers for our schools' funding. Though funding is not our main focus, we have been given money that we can give to our members. To date we have given our members in exchange for their $50 a year annual fee about $2 million, which is pretty exciting—that we've been able to sub-grant to our members.

Advocacy: we try to advocate for our members here in the government and in colleges and so on.

Communication networking: we want to facilitate the sharing of best practices, problem-solving between our member schools through our Web sites and other means. We develop products and other resources.

Data collection is important to have good data for grants and so on. We do that.

Accreditation: we partner with CITA—the Commission for International Transregional Accreditation—to accredit our schools.

Lastly, just like all the schools, all of you, NASS members feel tremendous financial pressure. In order for our schools to enroll 40 risky kids they need to make a transition from tuition to donation-based fundraising. Most are apprehensive about doing so. I didn't start a school to raise money. I started a school to be with kids. But you have to turn from that and you have to get brave and not be afraid to pick up a telephone. That's a whole other workshop.

So you have to do that and one of our members, Tanya here, moved up from principal to executive director. She knows she's going to have to get out and beat the bushes and find the resources that she needs, and so we teach that as well as finding money for our members.

We teach our members how to fundraise and speak to others on their behalf. And in addition, we engage in the joint funding ventures and approach nationally based corporations to find financial and other resources for our school. An example is we have volunteer basketball teams. We need money for refs. We need money for gyms. We need money to feed the kids afterwards. It may be the best meal they're going to have all day; and gas. One of our good friends is the president of a big company in New Jersey. We approached him. He gave us $10,000 to split between five schools so there's $2,000 each. So we very often try to find the resources that we need for our schools to survive.

I didn't start a school to raise money. I started a school to be with kids. But you have to turn from that and you have to get brave and not be afraid to pick up a telephone.

We receive grants from which we reward or sub-grant other members. In addition I'm always trying to be opportunistic and find new creative and replicable sources of income. We encourage our schools to be financially responsible and to maintain tight operations. We believe that our schools can attain high academic quality and with our help find the financial resources to not only survive but also to thrive.

Urban faith-based educational institutions are doing a tremendous job in serving the academic, social, emotional and spiritual needs of the children and adolescents of our Nation's inner cities. It is imperative that we continue to find the funding needed to keep them open and viable.

Now, Scott, what you said here about those that say we have to solve health care and poverty before we can solve education, we believe that we have to solve education, and then the solving of health care and poverty will naturally follow.

I have no doubt, with the right training, hard work, and vision and our God that we continually plead with and pray to, that we can develop the necessary resources to do so. Thank you.

B.J. Cassin

Good afternoon. I've been asked to give you our experiences in scaling up to high-impact models and I'm going to give a little background on the schools and then talk about that. My wife and I have been concerned about inner-city education, and our solution was to help with scholarships. But we felt uncomfortable. We were helping tens of people, but where was the leverage where we could help thousands of people?

And we all know what happens with the dropouts in inner-city schools. We've had lots of statistics today. There's more up there. In 2000, I learned about the first Cristo Rey School. And at the same time we were visiting some of the NativityMiguel schools and doing our due diligence. And we came to the conclusion that these two models could be replicated, and so, at the beginning of 2001, we put together a foundation that's specifically aimed at replicating these two models.

A little bit about the models and thank you, Mr. President. These are explicitly Catholic schools but are open to people of all faiths. It has a unique Hire for Work Program that I'll talk about, and the schools serve only the economically disadvantaged. The schools themselves love to say this in their local communities, "We are the most exclusive school in town. If you can afford the tuition, you don't qualify." Think about it.

These schools serve only the economically disadvantaged. The schools themselves love to say this in their local communities, "We are the most exclusive school in town. If you can afford the tuition, you don't qualify."

Rigorous college prep: Each of these kids when they come in is expected to go to college. Another key point of these schools and the NativityMiguel schools, too, is that these are independent schools in their locale. And once they're launched, they are running those schools.

A little bit about the Hire for Ed Program. All students work five full days a week and basically what it is is job sharing. They do not miss any classes. And, for the employer, we take care of all the government forms that have to be filed. These are typical jobs. The highest turnover rate in jobs in business is in the entry-level jobs.

And just think of a freshman. When a school opens, it opens one year at a time, freshmen first, so you've got a 15-year-old that's going on the 25th floor of a Boston law firm delivering mail, faxing, copying, whatever you may have. And today, there are over 1,000 employers of these students, and the job retention rate is over 90 percent. So, in other words, these are real jobs.

When we go to look to secure a job for a school and they say, "We'll do a make-work and consider it a donation," that's not a job, and we do not accept those kinds of jobs.

Amazing program impact (Figure 12): Basically, the income from the job goes to the school, so, in essence, the student is earning 70 percent of the cost of his education.

We are getting these young men and women into areas like the downtown that they've never visited and the 26th floor of an office building and relating to other people, their supervisor and, after a while, their co-workers, and they very much interact with each other.

"So we are doing budgets. Maybe that's why we have to learn math. There are lots of e-mails and lots of reports. Maybe that's what English comp is all about."

In effect, we made a $450 million endowment fund. This is last fiscal year's income where we raised $22.5 million.

After eight years there are now 19 schools. We opened six last fall—one here in Washington, Don Bosco, and a Cristo Rey Jesuit in Baltimore.

Various statistics: We are here to serve the poor. We have three more schools that are scheduled to open next year and four feasibility studies are currently under way. And please remember: 99 percent of those kids who graduated in 2007 today are in college, mostly in four-year colleges. These are two- and four-year colleges.

NativityMiguel: You cannot be successful in high school unless you are prepared. You've experienced learning. You've had the joy of learning even though it may have been pounded into you on Saturday morning. So NativityMiguel schools are small schools. It's an 11-month program, 7:30 to 5:00, two meals, summer program. Some of these kids who have never been out of the city are going up to summer class.

Another unique feature of NativityMiguel is these kids are followed into high school to make sure they're successful and actually now are being followed in college (Figure 13). Today there are over 64 of these schools. There were 17 when we started in 2001, and 90 percent of the students qualify for free and reduced-price lunch. So, we are serving the demographics. Remember that 92 percent of these students who go to a NativityMiguel school are graduating. And these are in areas of 50 and 60 percent dropout rate. And those kids that then get into high school, 96 percent of them—we track them—are now successfully going on to college.

So the scaling thing: What was our approach? Really the feasibility studies, startup operating grants, and we too have a great partner in the Gates Foundation.

- Students earn 70% of the cost of their education.
- The work program helps students see a purpose to their education, gain self-confidence, learn about business, and become motivated to go to college.
- $22.5 millon will be generated this year from the work-study program nationwide. A $450,000,000 endowment is needed to create similar revenue.

B.J. Cassin, "White House Summit on Inner-City Children and Faith Based Schools," (presentation, The White House, Washington, D.C., April 24, 2008).

Figure 12. Program Impact

And the last key thing I think is feasibility studies. When Wal-Mart opens a new store, they find out where the demand is. Then they figure out where the store should be. Then they figure out the cash requirements to get the store opened. They find the leadership team and the rest of the employees and train them. That's what we do.

These are local teams, not consultants. We require a rigorous program on these feasibility studies. They typically take nine months to a year. But when the feasibility study is done and the school leadership is identified and the local community buys in, then that feasibility study goes to the appropriate network for approval. Once they are approved, then the resources of the network come to help them open up that school.

The Cristo Rey network is located in Chicago, and NativityMiguel is located here in Washington. And to me this is extremely important. They're small staffs. They are the guardians of the standards. Each network has its own 10 standards, number two being important. Whom do we serve? The poor.

There's a lot to be learned. Collaboration, we talked about that earlier. What are the best practices? There have been faculty brought together ... not "How can we teach English better?" or "How can we teach math better?" but "How do we better understand the kids in front of us and what they face and what they're going through, and how can we respond and be better deliverers of that education?"

For the philanthropists in the crowd: invest in proven models. Only work with strong, strong partners.

There are 21 religious orders that are sponsoring the Cristo Rey high schools. There are 29 religious orders sponsoring the 64 middle schools. A number of these are joint ventures, so what these two models have done is provide a platform for people who've been delivering quality Catholic education for 100 years in the United States to go into the inner-city without having to worry about writing a check, without worrying about having to supply three nuns, four brothers, two priests.

And for the incredible religious orders, they saw dwindling numbers, and most of them did something about it, and that is train laity—train laity in their parishes in their method of teaching and where their mission was.

We are big on outcome data. We have the benefit of starting from one school, as opposed to trying to go back and get outcome data. But it's been said on this podium early this morning funders should demand data. The parents should demand outcome data. The teachers should. And we put it up on our Web site. Some of it early on and maybe even today is ugly, but at least it identifies something that we've got to work on.

- 64 NativityMiguel Schools serving over 4,300 middle school-age boys and girls in 27 states.
- 90% of students qualify for Free and Reduced-price Lunch.
- 53% of the students are African American; another 37% are Latino.
- 92% of these students graduate from high school, as compared to the national rate for African-American and Latino students of 55%.
- 96% of our high school graduates enrolled in a two- or four-year college this fall.

B.J. Cassin, "White House Summit on Inner-City Children and Faith Based Schools," (presentation, The White House, Washington, D.C., April 24, 2008).

Figure 13. Impact of the NativityMiguel Schools

And I think another key is sustainability. And the sustainability is the networks, what they can do for the schools once they open. And there's been a lot of passion on this stage this morning and this afternoon. And the real heroes—if you want talk about action—are the priests, brothers, sisters, lay people, men and women, ACE volunteers, the Jesuit volunteers. They have tremendous passion for these kids, and they respond. And the points I asked you to remember, those outcomes and graduation rates, that's a by-product of not only the model but also of the dedication of the heroes of these schools. Thank you.

Reverend Timothy Scully

Thanks, B.J. What a perfect time to celebrate this summit. We just celebrated Easter a couple weeks ago, and Jews are celebrating Passover this week. I'm reminded that we are all people who have eyes to find, in the darkest of places, hope. Moreover, these dark places can even be causes for celebration. So whatever your faith tradition, I suspect we are all here because we know only too well the grim statistics facing many of our inner-city schools, and we are bracing ourselves for another round of school closures.

But forgive me a question at the back end of Easter. Have the grim statistics become so familiar to us that we've forgotten that its ending is not inevitable? Might we dare to catch a glimpse of the vision that inspired Benedict here in Washington only last week to call these schools an outstanding sign of hope where no child should be denied a right to an education in faith, which in turn nurtures the soul of a nation?

Today my remarks issue from a conviction that our schools can and must be strong in our nation's third century. And they issue from an equally strong conviction that my business, higher education, must play a decisive role in sustaining and strengthening these schools, which, despite the recent losses, remain the largest, most effective private school system in the world.

> **My remarks issue from a conviction that our schools can and must be strong in our nation's third century. And they issue from an equally strong conviction that my business, higher education, must play a decisive role in sustaining and strengthening these schools.**

Universities possess three core missions: teaching, research, and service. Let me, in the time I have remaining, outline three strategies to address these three areas that we've undertaken in the northern woods of Indiana.

First of all, teaching—our leadership formation if I can. Despite the virtual disappearance of the heroic men and women who gave their lives to build the world's most remarkable faith-based school system, I'm absolutely convinced that we need not have a vocation or leadership crisis in these schools. The leaders are here. They just changed in appearance.

The young people who can and are able to lead these national treasures, as Margaret Spellings called them, are among us, and we have only to invite them to respond and offer them a distinctively faith-based formation. Sadly, of our nation's 240 Catholic colleges and universities, only one in five has built any program to form teachers and leaders for this bastion of hope. We can do more.

After two decades of practically ignoring the problem ourselves, Notre Dame created ACE in 1993 to help respond to this invitation. ACE prepares nearly 200 teachers and 100 principals to serve every year in communities across our country. In the past decade and a half we formed over 1,000 school leaders, and 75 percent of them are still in our inner-city schools, well beyond that two-year commitment.

That's a reason you should know about. We've been greatly helped by partnerships in building this effort. After all, let me mention two. First of all, AmeriCorps supplies us with needed resources and loan forgiveness for our recent college graduates, and I know a number of us have taken advantage of that wonderful institution that Steve Goldsmith leads so well.

Secondly, over the past 15 years, other faith-based universities, not just Catholic, have joined our efforts, forming teachers to serve the needs of at-risk faith-based schools (Figure 14). So together across America, this partnership is providing more than 500 talented and well-trained teachers each year in over 60 cities in 30 States. We must do more.

Imagine what's possible if we can harness the energy of these young leaders. So we've invited our thousand graduates and their young allies into what we call the ACE fellowship. Ours is no longer a two-year service program. Ours is a movement, a national faith-based leadership corps in service to our inner-city schools. The ACE fellowship is provided in 20 cities, working to transform inner-city schools and deepen our faith in the process. We need new ideas and white hot passion. And these leaders with the right formation and support are just the people to give it.

Third, articulating a compelling value proposition. Higher education must provide incentives to scholars to conduct research on the broad set of problems that beset our schools. Compared to the tremendous amount of resources directed elsewhere, these resources are virtually absent when it comes to supporting rigorous scholarship on faith-based schools. And without the ongoing research on school effectiveness and improvement, it will become increasingly difficult to make the case for our schools, let alone improve them. We must rearticulate the value proposition and disseminate it for faith-based schools, compelling reasons why folks ought to make the sacrifice to send their children to us. And the philanthropic community must help us provide such incentives.

So to arrest the absence of this empirical research, we propose to catalyze, together with my friend, Joe O'Keefe, and others a field of faith-based education. A few months ago our friend, Lee Shulman of the Carnegie Foundation, convened a national conversation in Palo Alto with leaders from faith-based schools across the land. And we emerged from that meeting with an ambitious agenda and a common one. At Notre Dame we are creating a center for research on faith-based schools and conducting research in areas like accessing public title funds that Secretary Spellings spoke about today.

Ours is no longer a two-year service program. Ours is a movement, a national faith-based leadership corps in service to our inner-city schools.

Technology in the professional development of teachers: How can we get more than 3 percent of Latino families to send their children to our schools? Our particular niche is certainly Catholic schools, but our intention is not to be parochial or isolated. Still, only if we compellingly articulate a rigorous and empirically founded value proposition will we attract more students to our schools and attract the resources to make them accessible to those who need them the most.

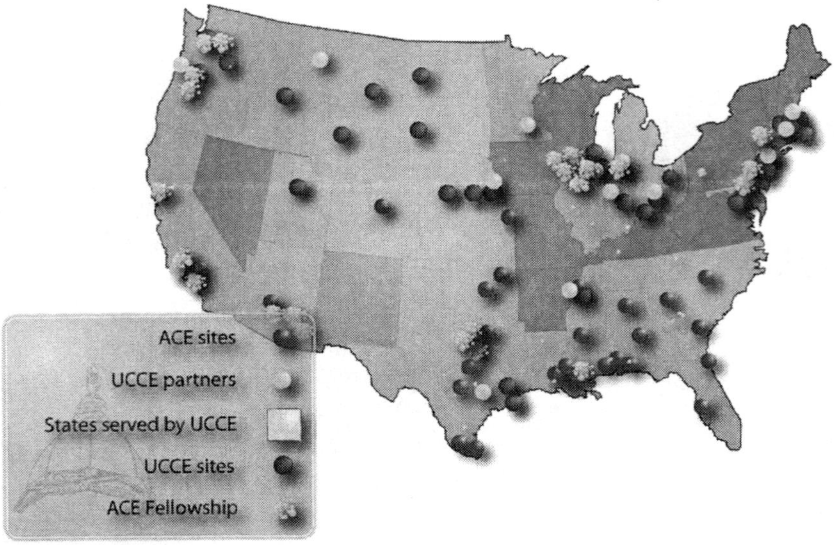

Reverend Timothy Scully, "White House Summit on Inner-City Children and Faith Based Schools," (presentation, The White House, Washington, D.C., April 24, 2008).

Figure 14. ACE SITES

Finally, service, or what we might, in agreeing with President Bush call "entrepreneurial" outreach activities. Universities can develop and have developed partnerships, direct partnerships with at-risk schools because at-risk schools often lack effective business practices. School administrators do amazing work educating children, but ours sometimes lack financial training. No board, no marketing plan, falling enrollment, and they don't know where to turn for help. Many schools consult consulting firms, fine. But they're too expensive for the very schools that need them most.

Therefore we've launched ACE Consultant, a not-for-profit organization to improve management practices in these schools. We believe that higher education is uniquely poised to marshal networks of national resources and expertise and hope to find partners in this initiative.

> **The crisis we currently face is ultimately a crisis of imagination and will. That's good news because we don't lack imagination and will. Together we can and we will succeed. We know the dark statistics. We know the gloomy trends. And it's important that we know them and acknowledge them if we are going to right them. But let us not get so used to the darkness that we fail to see the light. Signs of hope abound if we have the imagination and the will to see them.**

In addition, drawing upon some models we've heard about today, Notre Dame has partnered with struggling schools and seeks to develop a model to achieve thriving, sustainable parish schools. We call these Magnificat schools and currently have three, one just down the steps here from the Capitol, Holy Redeemer, one in Chicago, and one in South Bend. Our hope is to have Magnificat schools become beacons of hope and catalysts of innovation and excellence across the country.

These are some of the initiatives we are undertaking. In the end, the crisis we currently face is ultimately a crisis of imagination and will. And that's good news because we don't lack imagination and will in this room. Together we can and we will succeed. We know the dark statistics. We know the gloomy trends. And it's important that we know them and acknowledge them if we are going to right them. But let us not get so use to the darkness that we fail to see the light. Signs of hope abound if we have the imagination and the will to see them.

RABBI DAVID ZWIEBEL

All I can say is I'm so humbled to be part of well, this inspired summit obviously, but this panel in particular. The accomplishments and achievements of the programs that have been outlined in these few minutes that we've had an opportunity to listen to are just remarkable, and they're touching the lives of so many people. And it's really a privilege and an honor to be part of this group.

I've been asked to speak a little bit about the role of philanthropy in the overall upkeep of our faith-based schools across the country, with particular focus on the experience of the Jewish community and the Orthodox Jewish community, which is my particular area of exposure and knowledge. So let me start by spending a moment talking a little bit about the Jewish schools and what makes them similar in many ways to faith-based schools in other communities and perhaps what makes them unique in certain ways.

When we speak about Jewish schools in the United States, we are speaking primarily about Orthodox Jewish schools. For although the Orthodox community comprises, according to most studies, approximately 10 percent of the overall Jewish population in the United States, a large, large majority, approximately 80 percent of the Jewish schools across the country, are under Orthodox auspices. And that is the subject of interesting comments which I won't get into in any detail today. But one of unique aspects of the fact that the large majority of the schools are under Orthodox auspices and the large majority of parents who choose to send their children to Jewish schools are Orthodox is that the tuition burdens are quite substantial.

The typical school day in most of these Jewish schools runs from early in the morning until late in the afternoon because there's a dual program of instruction, generally religious studies in the mornings and general studies in the afternoon. And so my fifth-grader was coming home as late as 5:30 or even 6:00 at the end of a very long school day.

The tuition ranges in these schools, depending on the populations they serve and the areas in which they are located, from approximately $5,000 to $18,000 a year, and that pays for the dual curriculum that I spoke of before. And because families in the Orthodox part of the Jewish community tend to be larger and their income levels tend to be lower than that of the larger Jewish community, the tuition burdens are in fact way beyond what most parents can pay.

So according to a routine study, some 57 percent of schools' operating budgets are covered by tuition. And I assume that's not terribly different than it is in many faith-based communities or in some cases even less.

So where does the rest of the money come from? We know that government is not a major player in this area. It cannot be a major player because of the principles of separation of church and State. It cannot or it does not want to be a major player because of political considerations, whatever it may be, but government is, I would say, a minor player in the larger picture of supporting these schools. So then where do you make up the gap? And the answer ultimately comes down to private philanthropy.

> **If we recognize that our schools are not merely goods that are to be consumed by consumers, but that they are communal assets, then every single member of the community has a stake in the well-being of these schools.**

And we all know about the individual school-based levels. And I'm not about to scoff at the bake sales that were mentioned earlier this morning. It's one means of bringing in new funds, and obviously there are far more sophisticated ways, annual banquets and planned giving and all the different types of methods, all the different things we know are the retail business of fundraising at the school level.

But then there are also certain larger—I'll call them wholesale—approaches that are not designed to fund any particular school but schools in general. And again, these are some examples from the Jewish community which might be replicable, which might be approaches that exist already out there in the world in other communities. And maybe they don't, and maybe we can all learn from one another, and I hope we'll be able to follow up on today's conference with some of that "pollenization" in terms of raising funds for our schools.

One of the programs that I'm very excited about is Chicago-based, where the Association for Torah Advancement in Chicago has established something called the Kehillah Jewish Education Fund, in which every member of the community is encouraged to become a member and make a monthly contribution to this fund so that the idea is if you're a tuition-paying parent, you're a consumer of a good and a service.

But if we recognize that our schools are not merely goods that are to be consumed by consumers but they are communal assets, then every single member of the community has a stake in the well-being of these schools. And so we turn to every member of the community in Chicago through the Kehillah Jewish Education Fund and say, "Contribute what you can."

And over the past year or two, approximately a thousand families have joined this fund and have contributed close to a million dollars, which are distributed among the nine area Orthodox Jewish schools, most of it toward regular education per capita. And every school gets its per capita share of the total fund, with certain money being set aside specifically for special education purposes.

Another Chicago-based idea is starting to catch on, and that's the 5 percent mandate. It's the brainchild of a very active gentleman who was supposed to be here with us today, but I think he couldn't make it, Mr. George Hanus. And George has set up a program in which he's saying every Jew in their will should set aside 5 percent of his estate to Jewish education, to a Jewish day school of your choice. And every single member of the community is encouraged to set aside 5 percent of his estate for that purpose.

Targeting larger givers through matching grant programs: There's a foundation called the Avi Chai Foundation that was set up recently to be a matching program for first-time major givers. And in 2006, they brought in $15 million in additional and brand new funds into this program, which they matched by their own $8 million or so. And this resulted in grants to 160 schools in 25 States across the country.

So there are all kinds of different ways to encourage giving, whether at the grass-roots level or by targeting the larger givers. And by creating specialized programs which will be attractive to different types of givers. For example, in New York there's an entity called the Fund for Jewish Education, which has established funding for health and life insurance benefits for teachers in our schools and pension plans for career educators.

And this is such an urgent and important thing—to keep our staffs, to keep them and give them a certain basic level of security. And if you want to maintain someone's longevity in terms of our staff in our communities, we need to provide these kinds of benefits. Private philanthropy plays a major role in doing so.

So another example is capital construction. Happily, our community—you may have noticed the chart earlier where contrary to the trends in many parts or most parts of the larger society of which we are a part—our schools have been growing. There have been new Jewish schools built in recent years, the community is growing, and the recognition of the centrality of Jewish education has been growing in many circles. So we've expanded and added new Jewish schools to our rostrum.

And so we need money for capital construction projects, for renovation projects and such things. Again the Avi Chai Foundation has done wonderful work in this area, providing interest-free loans, five-year interest-free loans ranging from $750,000 to a million-and-a-half dollars. Over the past decade, they have made nearly a hundred loans through this fund, totaling over $80 million.

So this is the kind, again, of philanthropy which can make a world of difference to our faith-based schools. Bottom line is these are just a couple of different examples. There are many different ways in which private philanthropy can be helpful. In order for this to work, in order for this to succeed, you need to start with a certain baseline. And I think it's the baseline which is what today's conference, today's summit, is really all about.

It's the baseline of recognizing that, in fact, these schools are precious communal assets. You know, we heard the President say before that faith-based schools are critical national assets, and it was very impressive to hear that and very heartwarming to hear that. And I think if that were the mindset that prevailed in the larger public policy arena, I think things would change a little bit in terms of the policies that exist with respect to our communities.

> **If there is no message that emerges from today's summit more powerfully than the important and vital role that these schools play in our nation, in our families, and within our own faith-based communities, that itself will have been a worthy purpose for convening this summit.**

But they are also not simply a critical national asset, but as we have heard today, also a critical familial asset. The ability of a Jay Hein, for example, whom we heard earlier today say: we have two sons, and one of our sons is perfect for public school, but the other one needed a faith-based school.

Now, that's one of the problems and one of the shortcomings, I think, with respect to the Pell Grants for Kids program. You're eligible only if you're enrolled in a failing public school, such that the idea is not really empowering parents to make appropriate choices for their particular children, but just finding a way of getting kids out of public schools that are performing poorly. We ought to go beyond that.

We ought to at least recognize our goal. As Virginia Walden-Ford said, she has three children, and the first two were fine in public school. And they may have been very good public schools for all I know. But the third one just needed something else and something different, and that's the parent's ability, and that's what we want to encourage in our partners, to look at their children and find the best school out there for their particular child.

So these schools are a critical national asset and a critical familial asset. At the end of the day we need to recognize as faith-based communities that they are a precious communal asset. And if they are a communal asset, as I said earlier, the cost of supporting them must be borne by the community at large. And if there is no message that emerges from today's summit more powerfully than the important and vital role that these schools play in our nation, in our families, and within our own faith-based communities, that itself will have been a worthy purpose for convening this summit. Thank you.

Questions and Discussion

Hamilton Thank you very much, panelists. Like I said, the actual proves the possible. And after a day where we've talked about the struggles ahead and all that needs to be done, it is truly encouraging to hear of all the great success that you all have already had with what you are doing. I'm wondering, in the context of all the decline that we've been hearing about and talking about with respect to faith-based schooling in America, the numbers of schools closing and financial pressure, can you just quickly reflect on what you attribute the success of your program or school you have founded to? In this context of decline, why are you succeeding?

Mcdonald There are people who recognize that the inner cities belong to us all, whether we live there or not. And those children who live in these inner cities are our responsibility whether they're biologically our children or not. So what I've found is there are compassionate, caring individuals and groups who have stepped forward to fund and to save Catholic schools in the inner-city because they have worked for generations, and they want these schools to do it again, to just do it again. Do what you did for the immigrant population you helped before.

The inner cities belong to us all, whether we live there or not. And those children who live in these inner cities are our responsibility whether they're biologically our children or not.

Cassin In the 19 Cristo Rey schools and the 64 NativityMiguel schools, one thing I've observed is that there is a reservoir of people in the local communities that are ready and willing to invest in any of these schools, as long as they're comfortable with the model itself. They are approved by the diocese, each of these schools, but they are independent schools, and that, for the last three or four years, has been something that was important to a lot of Catholic donors.

Every school—you can pick a school at random, and there's a story behind it. And the story is one person gets involved and tells two more people and three people. And you saw the amount of money that the NativityMiguel schools raised: $53 million last year in 64 schools.

Is that sustainable? That's why we spend a lot of time. We have the president and the development director for every NativityMiguel school come to Washington for three days on development. And not only for the new people to have development 101, but it goes all the way up to how to choose a board, how to get the word out in the community, how to have a contract with your board member, what's expected of them. So there's a wellspring of people interested in supporting the programs. That's what we've found.

Tillapaugh It's a lot of hard work, I'm telling you. But years ago I had to turn my head from realizing a lot of us just need to be a kid sometimes, to just go out there casting the vision constantly and constantly identifying people. There are lots of people. In Denver alone I think I fund most of both my local school … the Denver school is running on $1.1 million and tuition pays for maybe 1 percent of that. That's just in Denver, nationally, obviously much more.

But it's constantly identifying, being opportunistic. And I tell my people, our members, that you're going to have to sacrifice; getting to be a good minister, to be with the kids, to be out there fundraising constantly. Compelling vision, excellent staff; I've got my fundraisers. I pretty much raised my own young ladies. I'll give you an example.

My senior development director at the Denver school came to me when she was 16 years old. She was a recovering cocaine addict. By the time she was 14, she was living with a 27-year-old drug dealer. She fell off the wagon and became a hard-core crystal meth addict. We had to let her go and get her in rehab. She had a powerful confrontation with God in rehab, came back, graduated, and started right away with computer data entry.

And she's an incredible individual donor fundraiser right now, getting a full-ride scholarship to Regis, which is a Catholic university, in business and finance. So raising them up and teaching them and having an excellent staff is a huge part of it.

Reverend Scully Well, Karl Zinsmeister is going to be furious with my response, but the truth of the matter is that the Holy Spirit will not be thwarted. And almost I'm surprised by the question. I'm surprised by the question because, of course, people are always going to be hungry for God and for an encounter with God. And so our whole success, if you want to call it that, is a response really deeply in the souls of the people who hunger for God. I believe that. And that is not going to change.

Rabbi Zwiebel It's a little bit hard to add anything to God.

Mr. Hamilton I think everyone will join me in thanking the President and thanking Karl and thanking Andy and the whole team assembled this day. And thank you to this fine panel for showing what is possible.

In: Disadvantaged Students and Crisis in...
Editor: Thomas G. Wilson

ISBN: 978-1-60741-535-0

Chapter 6

PANEL IV: PUBLIC POLICY OPTIONS

The White House Domestic Policy Council

DEPUTY SECRETARY RAY SIMON

Thank you. Welcome to a very special presentation this afternoon, the final panel of the day. My name is Ray Simon. I'm Deputy Secretary of the United States Department of Education. I had the extreme good fortune to have been educated in my local parish Catholic school from first through 12th grade. Although Sister Dominic and her fellow school sisters of Notre Dame had me on the fast track to the priesthood, other forces intervened, resulting in my spending the past 42 years as a public school teacher and administrator.

I believe strongly in public education, but I also believe that our nation and its children are best served by a diversity of schools, including specifically those that are faith-based. Faith-based and other private school graduates occupy many positions of leadership and authority through all levels of government and public service and are well-established in the private sector as well.

I believe strongly in public education, but I also believe that our nation and its children are best served by a diversity of schools, including specifically those that are faith-based. Faith-based and other private school graduates occupy many positions of leadership and authority through all levels of government and public service and are well-established in the private sector as well.

These schools have stood for and achieved much of what No Child Left Behind envisioned for all of America's schools: high expectations for all children, accountability for results, active participation by parents, safe learning environments, and high graduation and college-going rates.

Even though not required, a large number of private schools participate in some way with No Child Left Behind through directed instruction of children or professional development of staff. Many of these institutions provide extra tutoring for students in public schools who have fallen behind in their reading and math and, where permitted, have opened their doors to children formerly trapped in chronically underperforming schools.

I know Secretary Spellings earlier today reviewed her announcement this week to propose Title I regulations governing a number of important policy issues designed to make No Child Left Behind work better for kids and for the schools that serve and want to serve them. I would encourage you to review these proposed regulations and offer whatever support for them you can over the next 60 days' comment period, particularly those involving expanded opportunities for school choice and tutoring.

When growing numbers of faith-based schools close, shutting the doors on opportunities for hundreds of thousands of our children, we individually and collectively as a free society suffer. During this summit we have heard from a number of perspectives on the importance of faith-based schools and about the practical realities surrounding their continued existence. We've also learned of successful community initiatives to maintain their viability.

When growing numbers of faith-based schools close, shutting the doors on opportunities for hundreds of thousands of our children, we individually and collectively as a free society suffer.

We are now in the final presentation of the day where four distinguished panelists will consider the role that governments can legitimately play to help these schools and the students they serve. I will read a brief introduction of each and they will speak in that order.

First, Anthony Picarello. Mr. Picarello is general counsel of the United States Congress of Catholic Bishops, which he joined in 2007 after seven years litigating First Amendment cases at the Becket Fund for Religious Liberty, a nonpartisan, interfaith public interest law firm dedicated to protecting the free expression of all religious traditions. Before that he was a litigating associate at Covington and Burling in Washington, D.C. In 2007, he was named to the American Lawyers list of the top 50 litigators under age 45. He has discussed religious liberty topics in a variety of media and lectured extensively on religion and the law at conferences, seminars, and law schools across the country.

Next will be the Honorable Anthony Williams. Mr. Williams is currently chairman of D.C. Children First and chief executive officer of Primum Public Realty Trust. Mayor Williams served two terms as mayor of the District of Columbia, where he supported the enactment and implementation of the D.C. Opportunity Scholarship Program. Before serving as mayor of D.C., he served as the chief financial officer in the District. He served in the Clinton administration as the first CFO for the United States Department of Agriculture and has served in a variety of the other capacities in connection with St. Louis, Boston, and at Columbia University.

The third panelist is Ronald Bowes. Dr. Bowes is assistant superintendent for public policy and development in the Diocese of Pittsburgh. In this capacity, his primary responsibility is to raise tax credit funding through the Pennsylvania law called the Education Improvement Tax Credit Program. Over the past six years, Dr. Bowes has raised over $16 million to provide thousands of grants to needy students to attend Catholic schools. In 1990, he launched a large grass-roots network of parents and other citizens interested in advancing the cause of parental choice in education, the REACH Alliance.

The final speaker will be Lawrence Weinberg. Dr. Weinberg is author of *Religious Charter Schools: Legalities and Practicalities*, one of his many publications in the field of education policy. He has also written "The Legalities and Practicalities of Catholic Charter Schools," which will appear in the forthcoming book, *Catholic Schools in the Public Interest:*

Past, Present and Future Trends. Dr. Weinberg is co-author of an article with Dr. Bruce Cooper of Fordham University, including an editorial about faith-based charter schools, which appeared in *Education Week* in 2007. He was formerly a professor at Northwest Missouri State University and has worked as an attorney and consultant to numerous organizations.

It is my privilege now to sit down and turn the program over to our distinguished panelists.

ANTHONY PICARELLO

I realize I am coming to you about high siesta time and to talk about that most passion-inspiring of topics, the law. I will do my best to keep you awake. My pace might help. I've only got eight minutes.

Current judicial interpretations of Federal and State constitutional law have imposed substantial constraints on legislative and executive officials who struggle to respond creatively to the problems facing faith-based urban schools. Those constraints nevertheless leave important latitude for the political branches to act.

At the same time, the jurisprudence behind those constraints is in flux and may shift so that political branches have more latitude to experiment than in times past. At the Federal level, which I'll talk about first, the principal constraint is the jurisprudence under the Establishment Clause of the First Amendment to the U.S. Constitution, which reads, and I quote, "Congress shall make no law respecting the establishment of religion."

Current judicial interpretations of Federal and State constitutional law have imposed substantial constraints on legislative and executive officials who struggle to respond creatively to the problems facing faith-based urban schools. At the same time, the jurisprudence behind those constraints is in flux and may shift so that political branches have more latitude to experiment than in times past.

In 1971, the United States Supreme Court famously, in *Lemon v. Kurtzman*, decided a case involving an Establishment Cause challenge to aid to religious schools in Rhode Island and Pennsylvania. That decision infamously set out a three-part test for analyzing similar claims. That test has since been criticized, tweaked, restructured, occasionally ignored and even mocked, but nonetheless it has endured as the three-part "Lemon test." In brief, that requires that a law must, first, have a secular purpose; second, not have the effect of advancing or inhibiting religion; and third, not result in an excessive entanglement between religion and government. So it's purpose, effect, and entanglement—three parts.

The first part has never been difficult for faith-based schools to satisfy. They satisfied it mainly by having the secular purpose of ensuring that the citizenry is well-educated and to assure the continued financial help of the private schools, both religious and nonreligious alike. So each program satisfies that. It's a lay-up—no problem.

The problem comes in with the second and third elements, effects and entanglement. In recent years, the Supreme Court has analyzed effects in two different ways in school funding cases, depending upon the type of aid at issue, whether it is "direct" or "indirect" aid. To oversimplify these without getting bogged down in details, indirect aid is the kind of aid that is given out in the form of a voucher, more or less. The aid goes first to students and parents, and then in turn by their private choice, to the school of their choosing, whether public or private, religious or nonreligious.

If that aid happens to end up at a religious school as a result of the parent's private choice, then the Establishment Clause is rarely violated because the aid is directed to that school as a result of a private decision, and therefore it's not attributable to the government. It's not the government's choice; it's the parent's.

Direct aid, by contrast, is the kind of aid that goes directly from the government to the religious institution without the so-called "circuit breaker" of private choice—without it first passing through the hands of parents and students. And correspondingly, it is subject to stricter limits. In all events, whether the aid is direct or indirect, regardless of what box you're in, the aid has to be religion-neutral. What that means is, in effect, that the aid has to be offered without respect to the religion of the student or religion of the schools, public, private, religious and nonreligious alike. So that's that.

The third element, excessive entanglement—and again I'm going to oversimplify the subject—is violated when it involves the government in intrusive monitoring of the internal affairs of religious institutions, such as their finances, or government and religious entities work together so closely that the lines between the two of them begin to blur.

So these are the Federal limits. And what have political branches done to operate within them successfully? Two examples stand out. One is of course well-known to all of us, the voucher programs like the one in Cleveland, which allows parents of children in failing public schools to redirect public funds toward the school of their choice, whether public or private, religious or nonreligious. Remember, religion-neutral is the key there. And the Supreme Court upheld a program like that in 2002 in the case of *Zelman v. Simmons-Harris*, which became more commonly known as just the "Cleveland voucher case."

The second main solution has been one of tax credits. And of course we are going to hear about tax credits for scholarships in particular later, but these are individual tax credits that are directed to parents to offset the costs of various education expenses, like tuition, textbooks, transportation, things like that. That too was challenged and went to the Supreme Court in a statute along those lines that was passed through the Minnesota legislature. In 1983, the Supreme Court upheld that in *Mueller v. Allen*.

Now, one thing that's very important and worth knowing in this context is that both of these programs had to be tried and challenged before their constitutionality could be firmly established. And even now there are many questions at the limits of the Establishment Clause jurisprudence that new and innovative programs could help to raise and resolve.

In the meantime, there is an additional set of constitutional constraints that exist at the State level. Now on to the State level provisions that vary from State to State. Foremost among these is a group that I expect that you've already heard about this morning from Professor Viteritti and also thankfully from the President himself. Blaine amendments are State-level constitutional provisions that expressly prohibit aid to "sectarian schools".

These amendments take their name from James G. Blaine, a Republican congressman and presidential candidate from the late 19th century who proposed a Federal constitutional amendment that would have imposed this ban on aid to sectarian schools. It would have imposed it on all States as a matter of the Fourteenth Amendment, across the country.

As was discussed this morning, this was very, very popular but just barely failed to get the very strong majorities needed to get a constitutional amendment through. And because it was popular, even though it failed at the Federal level, it gathered momentum and ended up implemented in, as was discussed previously, about two-thirds of the States, estimates being from 29 to 37, depending on how you count or how you define a Blaine amendment.

Now, the language of these amendments can vary somewhat, and the gloss that the State supreme courts give to them can vary substantially. On one hand, they might end up being interpreted by the State to not add anything at all to what the Federal Establishment Clause prohibits.

On the other hand, they can be interpreted to mean a very, very aggressive separation of church and State, which at the margins can be so extreme as to get into different kinds of constitutional trouble. In other words, the separation of church and State can be so extreme that it represents religious discrimination that would violate the Free Exercise Clause, the Free Speech Clause, and even the Equal Protection Clause of the Federal Constitution.

So, for example, if a State were to provide an educational benefit to all students but then read the Blaine amendment so aggressively that it requires some students to be excluded simply on the basis of religion, then the State would at a minimum generate serious issues under the First and Fourteenth Amendments to the Constitution.

When considering a new legislative action to help shore up faith-based schools, keep in mind three sets of constitutional limits: the Federal Establishment Clause, State Blaine amendments, and State amendments, which limit the way public schools are funded and controlled. With all of these limits, the precise contours are unclear and the jurisprudence is in flux. It will require the right combination of courage and prudence to test those limits in court to expand the constitutional space where creative laws and programs can flourish.

In circumstances like these, Federal constitutional risks are increased by the fact that Blaine amendments were passed for the purpose of targeting religious minorities for special disfavor, particularly the denominational schools of Catholics and other minority faiths, to exclude them from government funding while allowing those funds to flow freely to public schools which at the time were very religious. They were just nonsectarian religious. These were common schools that taught the common faith. That's why the language of the amendments and the real hallmark would be the use of the term "sectarian" as opposed to "religious" more broadly, because that distinction bore a huge difference at the time.

So when a State applies its Blaine Amendment in the present day so that it harms the very same religious schools it was designed to harm back when it was passed, there again, that is the time when constitutional risks are at their height. Recognizing this, some States with Blaine amendments and with voucher programs have been presented with the opportunity to strike down the voucher programs based on the Blaine amendment but have chosen another way to strike them down instead that has nothing to do with the Blaine amendment. They sort of shied away from it.

Instead, in Florida, for example they relied on the "Uniform System of Public Schools" provision in their State constitution. The Colorado Supreme Court struck down the State voucher program based on requiring school funding decisions to occur at the local level. And similar provisions exist in different State constitutions all across the country, so some of it needs to be mapped out to assess where the risks are.

Now, it remains to be seen whether other State supreme courts, if and when they take up these questions, interpret those non-Blaine provisions in the same way. So to sum up briefly, when considering a new legislative action to help shore up faith-based schools, keep in mind three sets of constitutional limits: the Federal Establishment Clause, State Blaine amendments, and State essentially non-Blaine amendments, ones which limit the way public schools are funded and controlled.

And with respect to all these limits, bear in mind that the precise contours are unclear and the jurisprudence is in flux. It will require people with the right combination of courage and prudence to test those limits in court and so to expand the constitutional space where creative laws and programs can flourish. Thank you.

HONORABLE ANTHONY WILLIAMS

Good afternoon, everyone, and let me acknowledge the deputy secretary and thank him for moderating this panel, and I particularly acknowledge President Bush and the First Lady for really spearheading this initiative and this summit, and I applaud them for their steadfast support for the faith community and in particular for the role of school choice in promoting and advancing education for all of our youth. I think it's very important.

Also I want to acknowledge three people who brought me here. And who are they—or three groups. One is the Civil Rights movement. I wouldn't be standing here as mayor if it were not for the Civil Rights movement. I acknowledge our American government for ensuring an opportunity for all of us as American citizens. And my parents, who adopted me when I was four or five years old. I'm not quite sure when. I couldn't speak. They taught me to speak. I haven't stopped talking since then.

My parents made an important choice to send me to Holy Names School in Los Angeles. And if it weren't for the choices they made and their support for me, I wouldn't be standing here as mayor today.

But they made an important choice to send me to Holy Names School in Los Angeles. And if it were not for the choices they made and the support for me, I wouldn't be standing here as mayor today. I remember the Deputy Secretary was talking about his principal. We had Sister Mary Dionisia, who was the principal for seven years. And all I can say is she ruled before the time of the time out. She didn't understand about time out.

People often introduce me with, "Ladies and gentlemen, we have an exciting program, but first Mayor Williams." Or "Mayor Williams and the distinguished panel." When you're a mayor, you really have important functions in your city. Public works is very, very important. "Pick up the trash, please." Public support and public safety, very, very important. "Keep me safe."

But I think underlying all of that is something very, very important, and that's public education. And underlying public education, and I'm speaking of public education written very large, underlying that is really something even more important, and that's the notion of the public realm. When you're the mayor of a city, it's really your role to protect and conserve the public realm. And what do I mean by that? I mean all of us come into the public realm.

The public realm is not a physical thing. It's not even a temporal thing. It's just all of our contributions with all of our backgrounds and religious and cultural and individualistic [traits] in this public sphere, giving more than we get and leaving things better off than we found them. That's why we Baby Boomers are so well off today. All of our parents—they didn't talk about frequent flyer miles or where they sat in a restaurant or all that. They gave everything they had to make things better for us.

So when you're mayor, it's your job to leave things better for those that follow you. That's the notion of public realm and sharing and caring. I know that our mayor in Washington, D.C., cares about this and has worked with a great chancellor of our schools in Washington, D.C., Michelle Rhee. She actually assumed responsibility for the schools, recognizing the cardinal importance of schools and recognizing that parents ought to have the best for their children.

And that's why I, a former mayor, work with a number of different programs, including the Alliance for School Choice. I'm going to be taking on a tone from my fellow Democrats for participating in that. And then there's something called Fight for Children. Our friend Joe Robert has spearheaded an effort over the years to really provide opportunities for all children in the city, a public-private partnership, very, very important. And lastly something called D.C. Children First, which is really organized and focused on continuing the Opportunity Scholarship Program in the District of Columbia. And we are really committed to continuing it.

We are committed to continuing that program because we believe that it is important to pursue reforms in the public schools, no question about it. They have to be high performing and excel. It's also important to support our charter schools, and yes, it's important to protect and support our faith-based schools as another way to provide alternatives and opportunities for all of our children, to look at what's best for our children as opposed to what's best for various interest groups or various factions and to recognize the role that faith plays in our community.

Understanding the role of the Opportunity Scholarship Program is important. It's a federally funded scholarship program for low-income families. Scholarships are given directly to families without a lot of intermediaries. The tuition applies to any school, many of which are parochial and faith-based. And very, very importantly, parents, in many cases—let us face it—mothers in the most dire circumstances have an opportunity to make a statement about what's best for that child. And one of the things that's impressed me most as mayor is that mothers in the most dire circumstances will always, I don't know whether it's intuitive or instinctive or whatever it is, will know what is best for that child.

Now, has there been a lot of resistance? Absolutely, from leaders of both political parties actually. I don't want to get in trouble, but many leaders in both political parties, advocates and scholars around the country. We even had people doing color commentaries in other countries, commenting on the evils and the problems and the pitfalls of all this.

But what I believe is that, ladies and gentlemen, first and foremost, we are not about solving problems among the adults. We are about solving problems to meet the needs of these kids. I actually believe that these kids should not have to wait around until we actually achieve everything perfectly in our school reform efforts before things are being done for those children.

People ask me, "Well, how do you get this program now?" One of the things I say is, "You don't want to do this at home. It's very, very difficult." But I think there are a couple hallmarks of this. One, it was one of the areas where the Federal Government and the District worked together, the Bush Administration, the Secretary at the time, the District working together, local leaders working together, this mayor, Kevin Chavous. The leader on our District council remains a leader in these efforts around the country still. Peggy Cooper Cafritz, the head of our school board working with the leaders up on the Hill.

I could mention a number of them—one of them who played a courageous role was Senator Diane Feinstein from California, I applaud her for her leadership on this—got together and got a program tailored on the needs of these children, and very, very important, on the unique needs of the District government. And very, very important, organized a program, $120 million in new Federal funds over four years that did something very, very important, and that is it didn't take money away from the existing public schools, so we avoided this big ideological food fight.

The three-sector strategy provided new funds for public schools, for public charter schools, and for the choice schools. The scholarship portion has now provided help for over 2,600 children. It's serving the children most in need, with an average family income of $22,000. The vast majority would be attending a failing school otherwise.

What it really did is basically provided new additional funds, incremental marginal new funds for public schools, for public charter schools, and for the choice schools; let us say the parochial schools, the private schools. And it's now provided help for over 2,600 children. It's serving children most in need, average income of $22,000 per family. Standardized test scores in the bottom third. The vast majority would not be attending a good school but would be attending a failing school otherwise.

It's beginning to make a difference in test scores, although it takes time for these changes to take place, and I'm sure all of you can appreciate that. And I find it impressive that after just seven months, some scholarship students are already showing gains, particularly in math. Now, you can talk about statistics, but I'll just give you something that's very, very tangible to me and very important to me and that is talking to actual parents.

I had one parent tell me that "My child has never been so happy about going to school and actually learning."

And one student graduated from eighth grade and accepted the high school of his dreams. He said, "I've been given an opportunity to go to a better school with a better learning environment, a chance to be challenged and test myself in a way I never was in my old school."

Now, this has been a great program. It's having a real impact, but this program is up for reauthorization. And that's why I'm working with this effort called D.C. Children First, to see that this program is reauthorized, but even more importantly, to see that we attend to the needs of these children, and even more fundamental than that, to see that we recognize our responsibility and our commitment to the public realm and that shared space that's so important to all of us and very, very important to the future of our children. Thank you all very much.

Ronald Bowes

I'd like to tell you a story. As an attorney out in Pennsylvania, really in a certain sense it's almost as if we stumbled onto this. And I say that because we fought for school choice through vouchers for over a decade, and there were knock-down drag-out battles. I was out speaking almost every night. And I would go to panels in auditoriums like this at the various local colleges and sometimes in schools, the public schools, Fox Chapel High School and some of the others in the suburbs.

And they'd have panelists, and the panelists would be the ACLU, the head of the Pennsylvania Federation of Teachers, the head of the American Federation of Teachers and then me.

So it was always three or four, and actually every once in a while someone in the audience would say, "You know, this doesn't seem very fair. It seems like everything is against the poor guy who's trying to talk about school choice."

However, I always felt when I walked into the room that we were doing what was right. I always felt that I was able to select schools for my own children. I was a public school teacher, and in 1982, I was named public school teacher of the year in Pennsylvania. That's not to gloat—well maybe gloat a little bit—but what I'm saying is my heart and soul are with all children on both sides. But I selected Catholic schools for my children, and I believe that everyone, that poor parents, should be able to develop the souls of their children too, and that's why I joined in this effort for school choice.

In 1990, we formed the REACH Alliance, the Road to Educational Achievement through Choice. We would go demonstrate on the steps of the Capitol building in Harrisburg, constantly trying to get school choice done. And this REACH Alliance finally, with the help of ... Actually, Governor Tom Ridge was really the driving force behind this. And we really deeply appreciate his commitment over eight years to try and get some form of school choice in Pennsylvania.

I was a public school teacher, and I was named public school teacher of the year in Pennsylvania. My heart and soul are with all children. I selected Catholic schools for my children, and I believe that everyone, including poor parents, should be able to develop the souls of their children too, and that's why I joined in this effort for school choice.

But every time we would get to the precipice of passing vouchers—and I'm talking about 11:30 a.m. in the morning, the head of the Pennsylvania Congress would call me saying, "Ron, we have it, we have the votes." And then at 10 to 12:00 we'd see it slip away as two people would defect in the last moments, and we couldn't get it done. We came that close. Actually, Pennsylvania is still the only State in the United States to have passed in 1991 a full school choice bill through one house of the legislature. In other words, every parent in Pennsylvania attending a nonpublic school would have received a voucher.

It was passed through the Senate, but that voucher would have only been for $900. And the amazing thing about the program I'm about to tell you is that this thing is serving children so much better, and you can give them any amount of money up to the amount of tuition.

So with Governor Ridge's help and a strong grass-roots coalition and persistence ... We did kind of time it nicely too. We knew that the teacher's pension was coming up, and it was coming up for a vote, an increase in the teachers' pension. So Governor Ridge was able to leverage this at the same time. And the unions were so distracted and so intent on getting that pension that they figured, "Oh, that tax credit thing—we'll handle it later."

Well, they made a major mistake because once we got this tax credit program in ... and by the way, I would call this a pretax. It's not a tax credit. It's a pretax credit. And what's interesting about that is it avoids almost every impediment to school choice that you can think of. And I'll explain that in a little bit as we go on. But so committed leadership on the part of—at the time, when Ridge was governor, we all sat at a general assembly, and the House and the Senate were both Republican at the time. And the Republicans were more in favor of some type of program of school choice, which seems a little bit ridiculous to me, considering that Democrats are always saying that they're committed to the poor. Well, this program, obviously, is something that would serve the poor very well.

In 2001, we sat around the room and we devised the Educational Improvement Tax Cut Program with Governor Ridge and some of his public policy people. At the time we passed the bill, it was only $20 million and now it's 2008, the program is up to $75 million. $44.7 million goes to the scholarship side. In other words, that $44.7 million is for the nonpublic schools (Figure 15).

What we did was in that room back in 2001, we said "How can we bring in the public school sector and have them support this?" And so we came up with giving the public school Educational Improvement Opportunity money. And we did one-third of the amount of money that was set aside in the budget, in this case $22 million, $22.3 million was for educational improvement. So we built in this program where we could serve both the public sector and the private sector and that now has solidified the program over time.

Basically in a nutshell, the way this works is so simple an accountant can fill out one of these Appendix 1 forms in about 10 minutes, and he can send e-mail or fax it to the Department of Community and Economic Development.

And that was another ingenious thing. We actually put this not in the Department of Education, Pennsylvania Department of Education, we put it in the business-related section of government deliberately to keep out ideology, so we wouldn't have to worry about in another four years a change in administration or anything like that.

Basically, what happens is a business, a company can give, from its tax bill, they can divert it before it ever gets to the government, so the money never gets to the State. They are approved at the Department of Community Economic Development. They then write me a check. They send it down to me. I put it in the Scholastic Opportunity Scholarship Fund for Students, and then we divvy up the money based on eligibility and need, so we are able to serve all these children.

- $75 million cap
- $200,000 single company limit
- 75% one-year donation
- 90% two-year donation
- $44.7 million for scholarships
- $22.3 million for educational improvement

Ronald Bowes, "White House Summit on Inner-City Children and Faith Based Schools," (presentation, The White House, Washington, D.C., April 24, 2008).

Figure 15. The EITC Program in Pennsylvania

Over the years, over the six years of the program, we are up to $415 million. We have about 3,500 companies, and about 800,000 scholarships have been awarded. These numbers are incredible when you think about it. A family of one, the eligibility requirement is $60,000 a year if you have one child, and then it's $10,000 increments. So we not only give aid to the poor, but we also help the middle class, which I think is very important when you're trying to get something done. We also have a preschool program which has another $5 million separate from the other program.

And the amazing thing about this is that we have garnered so much money over the years that we have helped … there's a foundation in Pittsburgh, the Extra Mile Foundation. The director is here. Ambrose Murray, from the Extra Mile Foundation. Most of the money is raised through business leaders in Pittsburgh that see the value of a Catholic education. But they are now being helped by this, and they are able to use their tax credit money in addition to their foundation money, and it's a double dip.

Look at our diocese. This is one diocese, and we have 27,000 students, and we get about $15 million (Figure 16). We have over the last six years. In 2005–06, we had 800 students apply for preschool assistance that were eligible under the State requirements. Every single one of them had free preschool. They didn't pay a penny. And it was $3,500, the preschool tuition, so you can imagine how incredible this is, the impact on it.

I guess the bottom line of my presentation is that the corporate tax credit—and I say corporate tax credit, not individual tax credit, because there's even problems with individual tax credits, although I'm not against them, but I think the corporate tax credit at both the State level—and if we could do this at the Federal level, we could find a way to solve the problem of funding our faith-based schools. And so I ask you to go back to your States and to petition the Federal government that we get corporate tax credits in the United States.

It's a win-win for everyone, and especially if we put in this little element of educational improvements for the public school side, it will make everybody happy.

	Contributions K - 2
2001 - 2002	$2,008,895.91
2002 - 2003	$2,083,308.98
2003 - 2004	$2,149,304.00
2004 - 2005	$1,988,513.28
2005 - 2006	$2,015,960.50
2006 - 2007	$2,243,682.22
2007 - 2008	$2,424,550.00
Total	**$14,914,214.89**

Ronald Bowes, "White House Summit on Inner-City Children and Faith Based Schools," (presentation, The White House, Washington, D.C., April 24, 2008).

Figure 16. Entire Diocese of Pittsburgh Pennsylvania Tax Credit Contributions

Lawrence Weinberg

Charter schools are public schools that face greater accountability and have greater autonomy than traditional public schools. The school receives a charter to operate from a State-approved entity. It then receives a combination of State, local, and Federal funding. Forty States and the District of Columbia have charter school laws under which they educate over a million students.

The Establishment Clause requirement of separating the church and State applies to charter schools because they are public schools. However, the chartering process offers a faith-based school important opportunities because of the increased flexibility and control enjoyed by charter school operators.

The bottom line distinction—and I'm going to summarize everything I'm going to say in one sentence. The bottom line distinction is that a faith-based charter school can accommodate its students' and parents' religious beliefs, but it cannot endorse religious beliefs. Because the Establishment Clause draws a line that's far from clear, any list of permissible or nonpermissible activities that faith-based schools might engage in is not going to be perfect. Accordingly, these issues need to be discussed in broad terms.

A faith-based charter school can accommodate its students' and parents' religious beliefs, but it cannot endorse religious beliefs.

And it's important to bear in mind that these schools are always examined in their particularities and that every class, every prayer situation, every school board is going to be examined in its particulars. And the best example I can give of this is that the Supreme Court has held that a crèche in the public sphere in one situation is unconstitutional but in a different situation it may be constitutional. So the context and nature of the situation is everything.

Chartering does not permit a faith-based private school to close its doors at the end of the school year and then open as a charter school in the fall. Certain changes have to take place. And next I will address various issues of concern to faith-based educators that want to convert or hope to charter a school.

Staffing. There are changes that are going to be required in staffing. A charter school cannot have a religious criterion for staffing. Unlike faith-based private schools, the nondiscrimination requirements of Title VII apply to charters, since they are public schools.

Teacher certification. This really depends on the State. There are States that require charter schools to have all their teachers certified, States that don't require any charter school teachers to be certified, and States that require some percentage of charter school teachers to be certified. Some States permit alternatives to certification for their charter teachers, so it really varies from State to State.

Religious icons. Religious icons are not permitted in a charter school. However, it might be possible in a particular situation for a charter school to rent an existing facility that has religious icons from another entity, so the icons would be there but would not belong to the charter school.

Prayer. There are going to be changes required. Prayer must be wholly voluntary and student-initiated. A charter school may provide students with a room to pray in before or after school. It has to be the student's decision, and teachers and administrators cannot participate.

School ownership and management. That depends on the State and the Blaine amendment. If the State has a Blaine amendment, then you have to create a separate secular foundation. If the State does not have a Blaine amendment, you probably could have a religious foundation owning and operating the school within the other requirements.

Uniforms. Uniforms are permitted. A charter school can have a dress code and a school uniform.

Dietary restrictions, permitted. Charter schools may provide kosher or other religiously required food to their students.

Holiday arrangements. These are permitted. A charter school may close for religious holidays as an accommodation to their students.

Religious admission requirements. These are absolutely prohibited. Charter schools cannot have any religious admission requirements or preferences for students of a particular faith or faith generally.

Curriculum. That depends on the State. And what I mean is in terms of—not the religious curriculum—the overall curriculum, whether a charter school has to follow the State curriculum varies widely from State to State.

Religion courses. There are changes required there too. No religion course may endorse the religion being taught. You can teach morality. You can teach about religion. Or you can teach about culture. However, these courses cannot endorse the religion being taught. However, a course can endorse a culture or language being taught.

However, a charter school can rent space to a different entity that operates a religion course. And certainly if a charter school ends at 2:00, another entity can have a religion course that is taught at 2:15.

Board membership. It's open. Clergy may sit on the boards of charter schools, but there can be no requirement that clergy sit on such board.

Religious identification. A charter school cannot identify a faith.

Scheduling. A charter school can arrange its schedule to allow students to attend religious activities after school.

These schools are more than a theory, and next I'm going to talk about some charter schools. However, it's difficult to talk about faith-based charter schools for two reasons. First, some charter schools might be formed because parents had a religious objection to their local public example. For example, they might have an objection to the reading curriculum.

Now these parents may start a school, and that school may be 99 percent the same as their local school. However, that 1 percent difference—the fact that that reading material is not there—is going to mean the world to those religious parents that started that school. So I believe that is a faith-based school because these parents started it because of their faith.

The second reason it's difficult to talk about these schools is because a lot of the founders of these schools do not view their schools as faith-based. They view them as cultural-based or as language-based. However, it's important to understand that faith-based does not necessarily mean it's a religious school, and it also certainly does not mean that it is unconstitutional. Faith-based means that it is in some way simply based on faith.

And the following schools are faith-based to various degrees. The Adam Abdulle Academy in Rochester, Minnesota, was founded to meet the needs of Somali immigrants. The Ben Gamla Charter School in Hollywood, Florida, includes a bilingual and bicultural Hebrew curriculum. The Hellenic Classical Charter School in New York, includes the study of classical Greek and Latin, and many of those students then attend a Greek Orthodox school afterwards. There are two Hmong schools in Minnesota. I just two days ago learned about the Iftin Charter School in San Diego, California, which serves East Africans, Somalis, Muslim children. And though that school has an academic focus, what's interesting is that the teachers in that school are being taught about Islam so they can better understand the needs of their students.

Catholic schools in Washington, D.C.; Rochester, New York; Marysville, California; and Denver, Colorado, are considering or are in the process of converting to charter status, as is the Ross County Christian Academy of Chilicothe, Ohio. Religious leaders operate charter schools all across the country.

The critical point for religious leaders considering opening a charter school is whether they will be able to fulfill their desired mission through a school that can accommodate religion but does not endorse religion. And each religious leader is going to have a different answer to this question. And while I'm addressing in broad strokes some of the issues that religious leaders may have, these lessons can be applied in any number of ways at the school level, and some will be constitutional and some will be unconstitutional.

However, the fact that a number of charter schools are in operation already today that are in some way connected to a faith demonstrates that the chartering process offers a promising and realistic opportunity for leaders of faith-based schools who are considering ways of maintaining the viability of their institutions.

Appendix Notes

[1] Transcripts were edited and corrected to improve clarity and readability. For complete, unedited transcripts, see The White House, Education, "White House Summit on Inner-City Children and Faith-Based Schools," http://www.whitehouse.gov/infocus/education/whschoolsummit/index.html (accessed September 5, 2008).

[2] Harris Interactive, The Harris Poll, 2006, April 14, 2006: One-third of U.S. Adults Know Someone Who Homeschools Their Child, "Table 2: What Types of Schools Child Has Attended," http://www.harrisinteractive.com/ harris_poll/index.asp?PID=653 (accessed September 5, 2008).

[3] Alan Bonsteel, "Where Do Public School Teachers Send *Their* Kids to School?" in *School Reform News*, November 1, 2005, http://www.heartland.org/Article.cfm?artId=15818 (accessed September 5, 2008).

[4] *School Choice Yearbook 2007*, Alliance for School Choice, (2008), 2, http://www.allianceforschoolchoice.org/UploadedFiles/ResearchResources/Yearbook_Final.pdf (accessed September 5, 2008).

[5] Dale McDonald, *Annual Statistical Report on Schools, Enrollment, and Staffing: United States Catholic Elementary and Secondary Schools 2006-2007*, (Washington, D.C.: National Catholic Educational Association, 2007): 5.

MODERATOR & SPEAKER BIOGRAPHIES

(In order of Appearance at the Summit)

The Honorable Karl Zinsmeister

Assistant to the President for Domestic Policy, The White House

Karl Zinsmeister is the President's Domestic Policy Adviser, and Director of the Domestic Policy Council, which coordinates the domestic policy-making process in the White House. For more than a dozen years he was editor in chief of *The American Enterprise*, a national magazine of politics, business, and culture based in Washington, D.C. He was also J. B. Fuqua Fellow at the American Enterprise Institute, a major research institute located in our nation's capital. His studies and writing have covered a wide range of topics, extending from social welfare and demographics to economics and cultural trends.

Zinsmeister has published several books, including two Iraq War journals written during lengthy stints with U.S. troops in combat zones: *Boots on the Ground* and *Dawn Over Baghdad*. Prior to commencing work in the White House, he created a PBS film entitled "Warriors," profiling the men and women in America's fighting forces using footage he and a crew shot in Iraq.

Zinsmeister is a graduate of Yale University and did further studies at Trinity College Dublin in Ireland. During college he won rowing championships in both the U.S. and Ireland. He was an assistant to U.S. Senator Daniel Patrick Moynihan, has been an advisor to many research and policy groups, and has testified before Congressional committees and Presidential commissions numerous times. An upstate New Yorker, he is married and has three children.

Charles L. Glenn

Dean ad interim, School of Education and Fellow of the University Professors, Boston University

As Dean ad interim and professor at Boston University's School of Education, Charles Glenn teaches courses in education history and comparative policy. From 1970 to 1991, he was director of urban education and equity for the Massachusetts Department of Education.

Dean Glenn is the author of a number of books, including the historical study *The Myth of the Common School* (1988, 2002), *Choice of Schools in Six Nations* (1989), *Educational Freedom in Eastern Europe* (1994, 1995), *Educating Immigrant Children: Schools and Language Minorities in Twelve Nations* (1996), *The Ambiguous Embrace: Government and Faith based Schools and Social Agencies* (2000), and, with Jan De Groof, *Balancing Freedom, Autonomy, and Accountability in Education* (2004).

Active in education policy debates in the United States and Europe, Dean Glenn is a member of the boards of the European Association for Education Law and Policy and the Council for American Private Education. He has served as a consultant to the Russian and Chinese education authorities, advised States and cities across the United States and been an expert witness in federal court cases on school finance, desegregation, bilingual education, and church-state separation. Dean Glenn is the father of seven children, all of whom attended the Boston Public Schools. He holds an Ed.D. from Harvard University and a Ph.D. from Boston University.

Joseph P. Viteritti

Blanche D. Blank Professor of Public Policy and Director, Graduate Program in Urban Affairs, Hunter College, City University of New York

An expert in education policy and the role of religion in public life, Viteritti has published nine books and more than 100 scholarly articles. Most recently, he authored *The Last Freedom: Religion from the Public School to the Public Square* (Princeton University Press). He is also the author of *Choosing Equality: School Choice, the Constitution, and Civil Society* (Brookings Institution Press), which is widely recognized as an influential work on the subject of school choice. He has written widely on public policy, governance and law. Viteritti previously served as special assistant to the Chancellor of Schools in New York City and as a senior advisor to the Superintendents of Schools in Boston and San Francisco. He has taught at Princeton University, New York University, and Harvard University.

William Jeynes

Professor of Education, California State University, Long Beach Non-resident Scholar, Baylor University

William Jeynes has written numerous books and articles on religious education and educational history. His most recent book, *American Educational History: School, Society, and the Common Good*, was published in January 2007. His articles have appeared in *Teacher's College Record*, two Harvard University journals, *Elementary School Journal*, *Cambridge Journal of Education*, *Journal of Negro Education* and many other academic journals. Jeynes has worked with the Harvard Family Research Project and is a member of the International Network of Scholars based at Johns Hopkins University.

Jeynes is also a well-known public speaker, having spoken in nearly every State in the country and on every continent. He has spoken before the U.S. Department of Education, the U.S. Department of Justice and foreign leaders. Jeynes has received various awards and honors, including the Rosenberger Award at the University of Chicago and admission into Marquis' *Who's Who in the World*. He holds graduate degrees from Harvard University and the University of Chicago. Jeynes and his wife, Hyelee, have been married for 22 years and have three children.

Reverend Floyd H. Flake

Senior Pastor, Greater Allen A.M.E. Cathedral of New York
President, Wilberforce University
Former U.S. Congressman

Reverend Floyd H. Flake is senior pastor of the Greater Allen A. M. E. Cathedral of New York in Jamaica, Queens and President of Wilberforce University in Ohio. During his 30-year pastorate, Allen Cathedral has become one of the nation's foremost Christian churches and development corporations. The church and its subsidiary corporations own expansive commercial and residential developments, including a 700-student private school founded by Reverend Flake and his wife, Elaine.

Reverend Flake and the church have been profiled on CNN, CBS, BET, C-Span, PBS, and in *Time*, *Black Enterprise*, *Ebony*, the *New York Times* and many other publications. He is a regular lecturer in corporate settings, policy forums and divinity schools. While serving in the U.S. Congress for 11 years, Reverend Flake established a reputation for bipartisan, innovative legislative initiatives to revitalize urban commercial and residential communities. Before assuming the pastorate of Allen Church, Reverend Flake served in various capacities at Boston University and Lincoln University in Pennsylvania.

Reverend Flake serves on numerous boards and is a Senior Fellow at the Manhattan Institute for Social and Economic Policy, an Adjunct Fellow on the Advisory Board of The Brookings Institute Center on Urban and Metropolitan Policy, and a member of the NYC 2012 Olympic Committee. He holds a Doctorate of Ministry from the United Theological Seminary and a B.A. from Wilberforce University. Reverend Flake authored a bestselling book, *The Way of the Bootstrapper: Nine Action Steps for Achieving Your Dreams*, and he and his wife, Elaine, co-authored the book, *Practical Virtues: Everyday Values and Devotions for African American Families*. His latest book is *The African American Church Management Handbook*. The Flakes are the parents of four children.

The Honorable Jay Hein

Director, Office of Faith-based and Community Initiatives, The White House

Jay Hein was named Deputy Assistant to the President and Director of the Office of Faith-based and Community Initiatives on August 3, 2006. He is the founding president of the Sagamore Institute for Policy Research, an international public policy research firm headquartered in Indianapolis, Indiana. In this capacity, Hein directed the institute's research portfolio concentrating on a range of community-based policies such as welfare-to-work, access to college, affordable health care and crime prevention.

Hein also served as Vice President and Chief Executive Officer of the Foundation for American Renewal, a public charity established by Ambassador Daniel R. Coats. Prior to taking the helm of Sagamore Institute, Hein was Executive Director of Civil Society Programs at Hudson Institute, including the Welfare Policy Center, the Faith in Communities initiative, and community-based healthcare reform.

Also at Hudson Institute, Hein served as Director of Hudson's field office in Madison, Wisconsin, where he conducted hands-on research and analysis in support of the State's welfare reforms. He also served in Wisconsin State government as a policy director. Earlier in his career, Jay worked in a range of leadership roles within Illinois State government. He pursued his master's work in political studies at the University of Illinois-Springfield and earned his B.A. at Eureka College, where he was an inaugural member of the Ronald W. Reagan Fellowship program.

Phylicia Lyons

Founder, President and CEO, School Choice Illinois

Phylicia Lyons directs School Choice Illinois, an independent organization devoted to the expansion of educational options throughout the State of Illinois. Previously, Lyons was executive director of the Illinois School Choice Initiative, a project of The Heartland Institute.

Lyons received a B.A. from the University of Virginia and earned a Master of Public Policy degree from the Irving B. Harris Graduate School of Public Policy Studies at the University of Chicago, concentrating in education policy. Lyons has lived, worked, and studied in Western Europe and parts of Central America, where she has contributed to the fields of communications, public policy, technology, corporate finance, research and consulting, international relocation, and inter-cultural relations. Lyons is fully committed to making school choice a reality in the State of Illinois and that passion encouraged her to found School Choice Illinois.

Reverend Joseph M. O'Keefe, S.J.

Dean and Professor of Education, Lynch School of Education, Boston College

Father Joseph O'Keefe is an internationally recognized expert on faith-based schools. Prior to becoming Dean of the Lynch School of Education at Boston College, Father O'Keefe served as Interim Dean and Associate Dean. He is co-editor of *The International Handbook of Catholic Education: Challenges for School Systems in the 21st Century* and is lead co-author of *Sustaining the Legacy: Urban Catholic Elementary Schools in the United States*. In total, he is editor or co-editor of 12 books and author or co-author of more than 35 articles and book chapters on Catholic education and education administration.

Father O'Keefe has been invited to give keynote addresses across the world and has addressed Catholic educators across the United States. He has been co-director of Selected Programs for Improving Catholic Education since 1995, and he directed the Center for Research in Catholic Education from 2001 to 2006. Father O'Keefe received the 2004 F. Sadlier Dinger Award for service to Catholic education.

Father O'Keefe holds an Ed.D. from Harvard University, master's degrees in education (Harvard University) and French literature (Fordham University), and is a graduate of Holy Cross. He received the Master of Divinity degree and Licentiate in Sacred Theology from Weston Jesuit School of Theology, joined the Society of Jesus in 1976, and was ordained a priest in 1986.

Vernard T. Gant

Director, Urban School Services, Association of Christian Schools International

In his position as Director of Urban School Services at the Association of Christian Schools International (ACSI), Vernard Gant is responsible for overseeing over 400 schools throughout the nation that target and serve minority, under-resourced, and urban children. Prior to joining ACSI, Gant and his wife were responsible for starting and running a scholarship program to enable moderate- and low-income children to attend private schools, starting and running two Christian schools targeting and serving low-income children in Birmingham, Alabama, running a summer camp for children and serving in the children's ministry in their local church.

Gant has also served as both a college and seminary professor where he developed a master's degree program for pastors and ministers. Gant currently serves on the boards of the Black Alliance for Educational Options, the Alliance for Choice in Education, the National Association of Street Schools, and the Life Skills Center, a charter school for high school dropouts.

Gant has been the recipient of numerous awards, including the Outstanding Young Religious Leader Award presented by the Inner-city Jaycees of Birmingham, Alabama, the Jefferson Award presented by the American Institute for Public Service and the Paul Harris Fellow Award presented by the Rotary Foundation of Rotary International. He was also named "Birminghamian of the Year" by *Birmingham Magazine*. Gant and his family reside in Colorado Springs, where he is now in his 30th year of urban ministry.

Virginia Walden Ford

President, Black Alliance for Educational Options, Washington, D.C. Chapter Executive Director, D.C. Parents for School Choice

Virginia Walden Ford is a National Board Member and a founding member of The Black Alliance for Educational Options (BAEO) and is President of the Washington, D.C. chapter (DCBAEO). She also serves as Executive Director of *D.C. Parents for School Choice*, which she founded in 1998 to teach parents how to raise their voices to advocate for a quality education for their children. In January 2003, Ford organized parents for a successful grassroots effort to pass the D.C. School Choice Incentive Act in Washington, D.C. The legislation ensures District children and their parents the opportunity to choose schools that best serve their needs.

Ford's community involvement is the result of a personal experience. As a single mother, she raised three children in Washington, D.C., two of whom graduated from D.C. public high schools. Because of low-performing schools in the D.C. public school system, Ford obtained a private scholarship for her third child to attend Archbishop Carroll Catholic High School. She then became an outspoken advocate for school choice and is the author of *Voices, Choices, and Second Chances: How to Win the Battle to Bring Opportunity Scholarships to Your State*. Based on her own life experience and, ultimately, on the successful campaign for school choice in Washington, D.C., her book teaches parents how to free children from failing schools.

The Honorable Margaret Spellings

Secretary, U.S. Department of Education

Margaret Spellings is the U.S. Secretary of Education. As the first mother of school-aged children to serve as Education Secretary, Spellings has a special appreciation for the hopes and concerns of American families.

Prior to her tenure as Education Secretary, Spellings served as Assistant to the President for Domestic Policy, where she helped create the *No Child Left Behind Act* and crafted policies on education, immigration, health care, labor, transportation, justice, housing, and other elements of the President's domestic agenda. Previously, Spellings worked for six years as Senior Advisor to Governor George W. Bush, with responsibility for developing and implementing the Governor's education reforms and policies.

The Honorable Roy Bernardi

Acting Secretary, U.S. Department of Housing and Urban Development
Former Mayor, Syracuse, N.Y.

Roy Bernardi serves as Acting Secretary of the Department of Housing and Urban Development. He was formerly Deputy Secretary, charged with managing HUD's day-to-day operations, a $32 billion annual budget and the agency's 9,100 employees. As HUD's Chief Operating Officer, Bernardi worked to meet President Bush's management agenda to improve ethics and accountability within HUD's programs and among its grant partners.

Bernardi formerly served as HUD's Assistant Secretary of Community Planning and Development (CPD), helping to develop viable communities by promoting integrated solutions to the challenges facing the nation's cities, urban counties and rural communities.

Prior to joining the Bush Administration, Mr. Bernardi was the 51st Mayor of the City of Syracuse, New York and is still affectionately referred to as "Mayor Bernardi" at the Department. As Syracuse's mayor, Bernardi overhauled municipal financial services, eliminated duplicative departmental functions and streamlined governmental operations resulting in significant annual budget savings. A promoter of urban neighborhoods, Mayor Bernardi also implemented a number of new initiatives to improve the quality of life within Syracuse.

Prior to his public service, Mayor Bernardi was a public high school Spanish teacher and guidance counselor. He and his wife, Alice, are the parents of two children, Dante and Bianca.

The Honorable Stephen Goldsmith

Chairman, Corporation for National and Community Service
Former Mayor, Indianapolis, Ind.

While serving two terms as Mayor of Indianapolis, Steve earned a national reputation for innovations in government. As mayor of America's 12th largest city, he reduced government spending, cut the city's bureaucracy, held the line on taxes, eliminated counter-productive regulations, and identified more than $400 million in savings. He reinvested the savings by leading a transformation of downtown Indianapolis that has been held up as a national model. By leveraging public and private participation, a once dormant downtown realized billions in new investment, thousands of new jobs and housing units and an increase of 20 million visitors a year. This effort was part of a larger city effort that saw more police officers on the street and the implementation of a broader $1.3 billion infrastructure improvement program. Prior to his two terms as mayor he was Marion County District Attorney for 13 years. Steve formerly served as Special Advisor to President Bush on faith-based and not-forprofit initiatives and chief domestic policy advisor to the Bush campaign.

The Honorable Nancy Grasmick

Maryland State Superintendent of Schools

Nancy Grasmick is known for her strong focus on student achievement, teacher quality, parent involvement, public school funding, and early care and education. Under Grasmick's leadership, Maryland's SAT scores continue to rank first in the College Board's Middle States region, and Maryland leads the nation in improving high school students' performance in the rigorous Advanced Placement program.

Grasmick's career in education began as a teacher of deaf children at the William S. Baer School in Baltimore City. She subsequently served as a classroom and resource teacher, principal, supervisor, assistant superintendent, and associate superintendent in the Baltimore County Public Schools. In 1989, Governor William Donald Schaeffer appointed her Special Secretary for Children, Youth, and Families and, in 1991, the Maryland State Board of Education appointed her State Superintendent of Schools.

Grasmick received her doctorate from the Johns Hopkins University, her master's degree from Gallaudet University, and her bachelor's degree from Towson University. Her numerous board and commission appointments include the President's Commission on Excellence in Special Education, the U.S. Army War College Board of Visitors, the Towson University Board of Visitors, and the Maryland Business Roundtable for Education. In 2005, she was appointed to the National Academies Committee responsible for *Rising Above the Gathering Storm*.

Grasmick has received numerous awards for her visionary leadership and is a frequent guest columnist in various education journals. Her successes have been featured in such media outlets as *The Wall Street Journal*, *The New York Times*, and the BBC.

Scott Hamilton

President, School Risk Management

Scott Hamilton is President of School Risk Management, an organization working to provide low-cost, high-quality insurance to charter schools and private schools in order to help protect and bolster their independence. He is also Senior Research Fellow at the Thomas B. Fordham Institute. For eight years he was the Managing Director of the Pisces Foundation, a San Francisco-based philanthropy created by Doris and Donald Fisher, founders of the Gap,

Inc. In this role, he created the KIPP Foundation and served as its President and CEO. KIPP Foundation has created and supports over 50 independent public schools across the country based on the nationally acclaimed KIPP Academies in Houston and New York. Previously, Hamilton served as Associate Commissioner of Education in Massachusetts, establishing and overseeing the Bay State's pioneering charter school initiative. He was recruited to Massachusetts from Washington, D.C., where he held posts at the White House, the U.S. Department of Education, the Edison Project, and the Hudson Institute.

Mary C. McDonald

Superintendent of Catholic Schools, Diocese of Memphis

As Superintendent of Catholic Schools for the Diocese of Memphis, Mary McDonald is responsible for overseeing all Catholic schools within the region. In addition, she has responsibility for the Jubilee Schools, eight long-closed Catholic schools that were reopened in the inner-city of Memphis. These schools address the needs of children and families in poverty and have become centers of learning for the community. McDonald's responsibilities have included developing the infrastructure for the Jubilee Schools and providing ongoing oversight related to funding and school operations. The Memphis Catholic Schools system has grown under her leadership and has the highest student enrollment since 1975. During the past five years, the Southern Association of Colleges and Schools (SACS) has accredited all Memphis Catholic Schools and has recognized the Catholic Schools Office as an accredited School District.

McDonald is an author and columnist for several local and national publications. She regularly conducts workshops and seminars in education, staff development, leadership, urban education, and related topics at the local and national levels. She has received numerous awards for her work in education and social justice. McDonald received her bachelor's degree from Immaculata University in Philadelphia, her master's degree from the University of St. Thomas in St. Paul, Minnesota, and her doctorate from the University of Memphis.

Tom Tillapaugh

Founder and Administrator, Denver Street School System
President, National Association of Street Schools

An educator with a heart for the inner-city, Tom Tillapaugh has spent the past 23 years refining and sharing the street school concept. During that time, he has not only offered hundreds of Denver's inner-city kids a second chance to earn their diplomas but also has helped to start street schools all over the nation. In the summer of 1996, Tillapaugh saw a decade-long dream come true as the National Association of Street Schools held its first annual conference in Seattle, Washington.

Mr. Tillapaugh received his master's in Education from Oral Roberts University and continues to pursue a doctoral degree in school administration from the University of Denver. He has been nominated to *Who's Who in American Education*, *Who's Who among American*

Teachers, and received the *Teacher Who Makes a Difference Award* from Newscenter 4 and *The Rocky Mountain News*. Tillapaugh was featured in *Education Week* and *Newsweek* and spoke at First Lady Laura Bush's Helping America's Youth regional conference in Denver. Tillapaugh has also served on Congressman Bob Beauprez' education policy advisory committee. Tom is married to Yvonne Tillapaugh and they have four children and four grandchildren.

B.J. Cassin

Founder and Chairman, Cassin Educational Initiative Foundation

B.J. Cassin has been a venture capitalist for over 30 years. In 2000, he launched the Cassin Educational Initiative Foundation to establish private, college-preparatory middle and high schools in economically challenged communities throughout the country. He is Chairman of the NativityMiguel Network as well as a board member of the Cristo Rey Network and Foundations and Donors Interested in Catholic Activities (FADICA). He was formerly a member of the Board of Trustees of Saint Mary's College of California, serving as Chairman from 1995 to 1999.

Before becoming a venture capitalist, Cassin co-founded Xidex Corporation in 1969, which achieved Fortune 500 status in 1987 with sales of $752 million and 7,000 employees worldwide. He currently serves on the Board of Cerus Corporation and several other private companies. Cassin graduated from Holy Cross College, is married, has five children, and resides in Los Altos Hills, California.

Reverend Timothy R. Scully, C.S.C.

Professor of Political Science and Director and Fellow, Institute for Educational Initiatives, University of Notre Dame

Father Timothy Scully earned his Ph.D. in Political Science from the University of California, Berkeley. As Professor of Political Science at the University of Notre Dame, his research and graduate teaching focuses on comparative political institutions, especially political parties. He has published numerous books and articles, including *Rethinking the Center: Party Politics in Nineteenth and Twentieth Century Chile* and co-authored volumes including *Building Democratic Institutions: Party Systems in Latin America*; *Christian Democracy in Latin America: Electoral Competition and Regime Conflicts*; *Democratic Governance in Latin America*, all with Stanford University Press, and in Spanish, *El Eslabon Perdido: familia y bienestar en Chile*. In 1994, he was awarded the Frank J. O'Malley Teaching Award for Excellence in Undergraduate Teaching and, in 1993, the Charles F. Sheedy Teaching Award for the College of Arts and Letters, at the University of Notre Dame. He is the Founder and Director of Notre Dame's Institute for Educational Initiatives, as well as the Alliance for Catholic Education. He is a Fellow and Trustee of the University of Notre Dame and a member of numerous scholarly organizations around the world.

Rabbi David Zwiebel

General Counsel and Executive Vice President of Government and Public Affairs, Agudath Israel of America

David Zwiebel serves as General Counsel and Executive Vice President of Government and Public Affairs at Agudath Israel of America, a national Orthodox Jewish organization. He also sits on the executive committee that administers the organization's advocacy and community service programs. His areas of professional experience include religious freedom, church-state relations, civil rights, private education, and medical ethics.

Zwiebel is a member of the national board of the Council for American Private Education (CAPE), a member of the New York State Commissioner of Education's Advisory Council for Nonpublic Schools, and vice-chairman of the New York City Committee of Religious School Officials. In 1988, President Ronald Reagan appointed Zwiebel to the National Commission on Children, and, in 2005, Secretary of State Condoleezza Rice appointed him a member of the U.S. delegation to Europe's conference on anti-Semitism and other forms of intolerance, held in Cordoba, Spain.

Zwiebel has authored *amicus curiae* briefs in a variety of judicial settings, including the U.S. Supreme Court, has testified before various legislative and administrative bodies, and has published widely in the fields of religion, law, and public policy. Before joining Agudath Israel of America in 1984, he was associated with Paul, Weiss, Rifkind, Wharton & Garrison. He holds a J.D. from Yeshiva University's Cardozo School of Law, a B.S. in Accounting from Brooklyn College, and is an alumnus of Yeshiva Torah Vodaath. He is an ordained rabbi and lectures frequently on topics of Jewish law and ethics.

The Honorable Ray Simon

Deputy Secretary, U.S. Department of Education

President Bush nominated Raymond Simon to the position of United States Deputy Secretary of Education, and the Senate confirmed him on May 26, 2005. As Deputy Secretary, Simon plays a pivotal role overseeing and managing the development of policies, recommendations, and initiatives that help define a broad, coherent vision for achieving the President's education priorities, especially those related to the *No Child Left Behind Act*. He also provides overall supervision and direction of programs funded by the Department. He had previously served as the Assistant Secretary for Elementary and Secondary Education.

Simon was the Chief State School Officer for Arkansas for six years—a position he held until his initial appointment by President Bush. He also served as superintendent of the Conway (Arkansas) School District from 1991 to 1997.

A native of Conway, Arkansas, Simon has been involved in Arkansas education since 1966, when he began his career as a mathematics teacher at North Little Rock High School. While there, he was also Director of School Food Services and Director of Computer Services until moving back to Conway to serve as Assistant Superintendent for Finance. In addition, he has been an adjunct professor of both educational technology and school finance at the undergraduate and graduate levels.

He received a bachelor's and master's degree in mathematics from the University of Central Arkansas and holds an educational specialist degree in school administration from the University of Arkansas. Simon and his wife, Phyllis, have one married daughter and two grandchildren.

Anthony R. Picarello, Jr.

General Counsel, United States Conference of Catholic Bishops

Anthony Picarello joined the United States Conference of Catholic Bishops after seven years litigating First Amendment cases at the Becket Fund for Religious Liberty, a non-partisan, interfaith, public-interest law firm dedicated to protecting the free expression of all religious traditions. Previously, he spent three years as a litigation associate at Covington & Burling in Washington, D.C., following a federal district court clerkship. In January 2007, Picarello was named to *The American Lawyer's* list of the top 50 litigators under age 45. He is admitted to practice before the U.S. Supreme Court and has argued religious freedom cases before federal district and appellate courts.

Picarello has discussed religious liberty topics in a variety of media. He has appeared on ABC's *World News Tonight*, C-Span's *Washington Journal*, Fox News Channel's *O'Reilly Factor* and other television shows. Picarello has been quoted in *The New York Times*, *The Wall Street Journal*, *U.S.A Today*, *The Washington Post*, and many other newspapers, and his opinion pieces have appeared in *U.S.A Today*, *New York Newsday*, *The National Law Journal*, *The Legal Times*, and others. He also has lectured extensively on religion and the law at conferences, seminars and law schools across the country.

Mr. Picarello holds a J.D. from the University of Virginia, a master's in Religious Studies from the University of Chicago, and an A.B., magna cum laude, in Social Anthropology and Comparative Religion from Harvard University.

Anthony A. Williams

Chairman, D.C. Children First
Former Mayor, District of Columbia
Chief Executive Officer, Primum Public Realty Trust

In 2007, Anthony Williams co-founded Primum Public Realty Trust, a wholly owned subsidiary of Friedman, Billings, Ramsey (FBR) Group, Inc. Prior to joining FBR, Williams served two terms as the fourth Mayor of the District of Columbia from January 1999 through December 2006. He served as the District of Columbia's Chief Financial Officer (CFO) from October 1995 through June 1998.

Prior to becoming Mayor, Williams was appointed by President Clinton and confirmed by the Senate to serve as the first CFO of the U.S. Department of Agriculture as well as a founder and Vice Chairman of the U.S. CFO Council. Williams also has served as the Deputy State Comptroller of Connecticut; the Executive Director of the Community Development Agency in St. Louis, Missouri; Assistant Director of the Boston Redevelopment Authority and Adjunct Professor at Columbia University. In 1997, *Governing Magazine* named him Public Official of the Year.

Williams graduated *magna cum laude* with a B.A. in Political Science from Yale College and earned a J.D. from Harvard Law School and a master's degree in Public Policy from the Kennedy School of Government at Harvard University. He also served in the United States Air Force.

Ronald T. Bowes

Assistant Superintendent for Public Policy and Development, Diocese of Pittsburgh

As Assistant Superintendent for Public Policy and Development for the Diocese of Pittsburgh, Bowes' primary responsibility is to raise tax credit funding through a Pennsylvania law called the Educational Improvement Tax Credit Program. Over the past six years, Bowes has raised over $16 million to provide thousands of grants to needy students to attend Catholic schools.

In 1990, he established a large grassroots network of parents and other citizens interested in advancing the cause of parental choice in education, the Road to Educational Achievement through Choicē (REACH) Alliance. Bowes remains an active member of this organization today. He has spoken on school choice and education reform in many different venues, including Duquesne University, the University of Notre Dame, Carnegie-Mellon University, the University of Pittsburgh, and Oxford University in England. In 2004, Bowes was honored by the National Catholic Educational Association with the Parental Choice Advocate Award.

Bowes holds a B.A. in Political Science, a master's in History from Duquesne University, and a doctorate from Carnegie-Mellon University. In 1990, he was inducted into the Duquesne University Century Club of Distinguished Graduates.

Lawrence D. Weinberg

Author, Religious Charter Schools: Legalities and Practicalities

Lawrence Weinberg is the author of the book *Religious Charter Schools: Legalities and Practicalities*, one of his many publications in the field of education policy. He has also written "The Legalities and Practicalities of Catholic Charter Schools," which will appear in the forthcoming book *Catholic Schools in The Public Interest: Past, Present, and Future Trends*, edited by Patricia Bauch. Weinberg has co-authored articles with Bruce Cooper of Fordham University, including an editorial about faith-based charter schools, which appeared in *Education Week* in June 2007.

Weinberg was formerly a professor of educational leadership at Northwest Missouri State University. He also has worked as an attorney and was one of the attorneys of record in a published New Jersey Appellate Division commercial law decision, *Parks v. Commerce Bank*. He has consulted with the William E. Simon Foundation, the Association of Christian Schools International, and Agudath Israel of America related to religious charter schools. Weinberg holds a master's degree in Education from Northwestern University and a law degree and doctor of education degree from Boston University.

INDEX

C

D

E

F

G

H

I

J

K

L

M

Q

R

S

T

U

V

W

Y